MARIANO BALLESTER

THE SECRET
LANGUAGE OF SIGNS

An Invitation to a Spiritual Reading of Life

Translated from the Italian
by Bianca Zagolin

MÉDIASPAUL

Originally published as *Fratello segno, sorella vita* by Edizioni Messaggero, Padova, Italy, 1992.

Canadian Cataloguing in Publication Data

Ballester, Mariano

The Secret Language of Signs: An Invitation to a Spiritual Reading of Life

Translation of: Fratello segno, sorella vita.
Includes bibliographical references.

ISBN 2-89420-080-3

1. Symbolism. 2. Life—Religious aspects—Christianity. 3. Spiritual Life.
4. Nature—Religious aspects—Christianity. 5. Symbolism in the Bible. I. Title

BV150.B3413 1997   246'.55   C97-940192-5

Phototypesetting : *Médiaspaul*

Cover : *Summum*

ISBN 2-89420-080-3

Legal Deposit — 2nd Quarter 1997
Bibliothèque nationale du Québec
National Library of Canada

© 1997   Médiaspaul
         250, boul. St-François Nord
         Sherbrooke, QC, J1E 2B9 (Canada)

To my dear brothers the trees
big and small;

to all the creatures of the forest;

to the winds, and the waters, to the earth and the sky,
distressed, tormented by our "progress";

to those angelic beings who care for them
with untiring love;

but most of all
to the angel of the four-leaved clover,
with humble gratitude.

TABLE OF CONTENTS

FOREWORD

In many aspects, this book can be viewed as part of a sequence that it forms with the previous two, Iniziazione alla preghiera profonda (Initiation to Deep Prayer) *and* Meditare un sogno (Meditating a Dream). *In all three, I show that continuous transparency of the different levels of our being is an essential prerequisite to understanding and fulfilling our true goal in life.*

One of the most wonderful and encouraging effects of this gradual transparency is receiving the special grace that enables us to read life in spiritual terms.

Through these pages, readers will understand that our everyday world is an endless source of messages, and they will find the appropriate means and directions to interpret them. As a further incentive, I have included various testimonies from those who have already gone forward into this marvellous quest which involves all the dimensions of a human being. I apologize for alluding so often to the events and experiences of my own life: it was the biggest obstacle I had to overcome in order to be able to write. However, I have understood that life is to be given and that it is better to open it up than to close it.

I am deeply grateful, not only to those to whom this book is dedicated, but to so many others, starting with the participants in my meditation courses and my friends who have richly contributed to the book with their personal accounts. I also wish to express my gratitude to my publisher who made it possible for this message to be spread, and for being so receptive to the idea of this new work as well as to the preceding ones. Finally, special thanks to my dear friend Rodolfo for his sustained help in the writing.

M.B.

INTRODUCTION

As a man who would have been carried in his sleep on an island, deserted and frightening, and would awake without knowing where he might be, seeing no means of escape... I tried to see if God perchance had not left some sign of Himself.

B. PASCAL

1. THE LETTER OF AWAKENING

The Forgetful Son

In an ancient Christian poem, we are told of a message sent by the heavenly sovereigns to their son who, in a distant land, has forgotten who he is. The purpose of the royal letter is indeed to awaken the young prince from his torpor, immersed as he is in a world of temptations, unaware of his lineage and of the sacred mission that has taken him to Egypt: to recover a precious pearl. The prince himself relates his adventures, which begin with his dramatic forgetting:

> I forgot everything about the Pearl for which my Parents had sent me on my journey; and, on account of their heavy food, I fell into a deep sleep.[1]

"The Song of the Pearl", as this poem of the second century A.D. is known to scholars, certainly echoes the well-known parable, told in the Gospel, of the Prodigal Son: his cycle of leaving home, then coming back, of going to a distant land only to squander his fortune, is similar to the sleep, followed by forgetfulness experienced by the young prince in the Christian poem, and both return to their father's home in a similar fashion.

But the prince's sleep is also the sleep and spiritual heavyness of every child of God who allows himself to be hypnotized by the "foods" of the world. These come in

---

1. Quoted in F.C. Happold, *Misticismo, studio e antologia*, Mondadori, Milano, 1997, pp. 200-205.

innumerable varieties and constantly appeal to us in an infinite range of possibilities, from the most material, coarse temptations to the more subtle, refined ones. This can be evidenced by the "spiritual pedestals" and assorted sweet-smelling incenses with which many like to adorn and sustain their little *egos*, the disordely attachments to people and things, the frenzied race for power at the top. The hypnotized mind, as in the case of the slumbering young prince, will take it upon itself to satisfy our every desire, skillfully and shrewdly, constantly shifting from one to the other.

If, as they say, man is what he eats, all the more so will a man, who regularly feeds on worldly and selfish thoughts, images and emotions, become colored and defined by the hues and the enormous power of those foods, which can penetrate and transform much more subtly than physical nourishment. Anyone can experience how dull and meaningless one's environment becomes when one is assailed by the thousand and one negative factors which today are usually referred to as "depression". Nothing, not even the most beautiful sight in nature or the happiest event, can arouse a depressed person.

Divine Attention

That is why the letter of awakening is needed. The kingdom of heaven, mysterious dwelling of our Father, cannot remain indifferent at the sight of so many of its children in the grip of all kinds of addictions, be they physical, psychological or spiritual:

About all that was happening, my parents found out and became concerned.[2]

The letter itself is a predictable reaction: the divine Father-Mother cannot forget his-her son on a mission. On the other hand, the sending of the letter indicates that somehow the parents have been "accompanying" their son, and it is precisely at the most crucial moment of his experience that they intervene with their message.

Some might think that the letter of awakening is pointless for a man deeply immersed in his torpor, as he has long since become insensitive to any stimulus that originates from a higher dimension. But that would be forgetting a central aspect, and much more, the most radically important one of man's entire existence: love. Every human being has come into this world to learn to love. The complex patterns of the human journey have no other purpose, nor higher, more essential meaning than to develop deep, authentic love, one and yet threefold, since the only genuine love is perceived in three dimensions when applied to God, our neighbor and ourselves.[3]

Now, the letter of awakening has no other purpose than to rouse man to his true mission, that is, to love. Undoubtedly, it shall be useless for one who is completely blinded and has deliberately plunged into the lies and illusions of worldly ambitions. Saint Paul says of these individuals that "they exchanged the truth of God for a lie" and "they

---

2. *Ibid.*, p. 202.

3. For Jesus, the commandment to love God, one's neighbor and oneself (Mt 22, 34-40) sums up the Old and the New Testaments. In the parallel text in Luke (10, 28), Christ adds the words "do this and you shall live", indicating that the true meaning and fulfillment of life can be found in the mystery of this threefold love.

became vain in their reasoning, and their senseless minds were darkened" (Rom 1, 21, 25).

We must remember that love is free, as the essence of life itself. Therefore, the letter of awakening is born out of love, is a call of love emanating from the heart of He who is Love above all. It is He, the mysterious One, who tries with every possible means to rekindle in his children, lulled into torpor, the spark of life-love that lies deep within the authentic self. After all, even if his heart is poisoned with worldly foods, man is not just an inanimate chemical compound, whose transformation depends on laboratory technology. He keeps in his heart that divine spark, the seed that is his birthright as a creature of God, but which may have been obstructed and covered with layers of dirt that make it invisible and inoperative.

Message and Signs

The following passage, full of beauty and shades of symbolic meaning, sums up the content of the divine message found in the letter:

We—your Father, king of kings, and your Mother, queen of the land of the Dawn, and your brother second-born—salute you, our son who are in Egypt! Awake from your sleep and listen to the words of this letter! Remember that you are the son of a king and realize that you have become a slave![4]

Such is the essence of the message that, in so many different forms, at any age and every day, God the Father-

---

4. *Ibid.*, p. 203.

Mother sends his-her children. And these infinitely varied messages are our brothers the signs; great and portentous or small and humble, enhanced with different hues or rhythms, they all repeat the same refrain: "Wake up, shake yourself out of your sleep and listen to the words of our message!".

This books aims at providing some help in reading these friendly messages that knock on our door every day. As I have already indicated, I hesitated in writing on this topic. My mind allied itself to my own laziness, providing all sorts of arguments to it not to write. I resisted for years, vaguely procrastinating on that fateful decision, until it closed in on me, forcing me to answer yes or no. But all the time, it was my little brothers the signs that mounted guard around me, never leaving me alone, until I would decide to write. No matter how hard I tried to ignore them, everything that I read, everything I chanced to see, the words people spoke to me, quite unaware that they were bearers of a message meant for me, it all boiled down to the same refrain: "You must write, dear, lazy brother! You cannot avoid it any longer! What is the point of putting it off any longer?". To refuse drastically hardly seemed the nice thing to do. After all, I always loved my brothers the signs, and they were the ones to help and guide me at certain cross-roads on my journey on this planet.

The problem was solved on a beautiful Roman July day (fortunately a cool one). At the end of a meditation, during which the little signs had whirled around in my mind in a mad turmoil, amusing themselves in leading it away from its center of silence and peace, the right moment came. I sat up, took pen and paper and started to write—this is unusual for me—right from page one: "In an ancient Christian poem...". Then a strange thing happened: inside me, as well as outside, I felt a vibration, like a gentle breathing, in which I could hear a symphony of little voices crying out: "Finally...!".

2. KNOWING HOW TO READ A SIGN

What significance can have the letter of awakening for us, men and women of a century that is marked by constant change in the structure of our lives and by the countless points of interest that incessantly solicit our minds? Today, the quiet reading of psalms and the quest for wisdom in ancient texts have been replaced by the busy production of endless data and news in the pages of our papers or on our computer screens, information quickly printed and read, only to be thrown out or filed and soon forgotten. Can an old parable about princes and kings really tell us something new, we who can see every day, in one half-hour of televised news, heads of state meeting, international conferences and the political and economic negotiations of democratic nations?

The answer is yes. However, its meaning depends on a secret: knowing how to read a sign. Each morning, as we wake up, we can be sure that a series of signs is awaiting to accompany us through the day, starting with our dreams from the night before, of which we may have but a blurry recollection. As we shall see, the important thing is to learn to become receptive to our brothers the signs, big or small, and to know how to read the messages they bear. Otherwise, as the ancient rabbis used to say, it is just as if we did not read the letters delivered by the postman.

But what is a sign?

It is interesting to note that both scholars and mystics agree on one essential aspect of the notion of sign: its otherness. A sign, they say, always leads to knowing *another* reality and thus invites us to immediately go beyond it. Saint Thomas, for instance, states that a sign is any reality that manifests another.[5]

Saint Augustine gives the notion an important theological dimension. Based on his definition of a sign as something that leads us to knowledge beyond its perceptible manifestation, we can apply signs to knowing divine will, to establishing the credibility of Revelation, to understanding the deeper meaning of the sacraments, etc.[6]

Sign and Symbol

Yet, the notion of sign must be distinguished from that of symbol. Indeed, it is precisely the concept of *otherness* that will provide us with the differentiating trait. A sign manifests "another thing or reality", often expressed in an arbitrary fashion, as in the case of mathematical signs. There is, generally speaking, no *natural* link between the sign and the thing signified.

On the other hand, a symbol possesses that link intrinsically: the richness of its meaning springs from its very nature. All we have to do is recall how numerous and deep are the meanings of the four symbols-elements: earth, air, water and fire. As a result, the meaning of a symbol is

---

5. Saint Thomas, *De Veritate,* q. 9, a. 4 ad 4: "Quodcumque notum in quo aliquid cognoscatur". Cf. *Summa theologiae,* III, q. 60, a. 4: "Signum est per quod aliquis devenit in cognitionem alterius".

6. Cf. *De doctrina christiana,* i, II, c. I: PL XXXIV, col.35.

multivalent and multidimensional, overflowing with richness, and it can even go beyond itself.

A sign is much more modest and limited: by its very simplicity, it points to only one thing, only one meaning. Therefore, it is also much clearer, more transparent than a symbol. As when Noah, after the endless days of the flood, sent out a dove from the ark to see if the waters had receded from the earth, he was given a beautiful sign, luminous, humble yet unequivocal: "Toward evening, the dove came back to him, and there in its beak was a plucked-off olive leaf" (Gn 8, 11). Noah understood the sign: mother earth was opening up to him once more.

A symbol is not always as clear. In spite of man's efforts, and even though he may apply all his intellectual abilities to grasping its various meanings, the symbol may most often elude him or remain ambiguous, even conceal its secret for centuries to the uninitiated. The visitor in Pompei will undoubtedly be fascinated by the magnificent frescoes of the Villa of Mysteries. He will admire the figures and symbolic forms of the initiation ceremony filing by on the striking red background; it is all rhythmical, precisely ordered, from the first ritual scene to the last, and yet, at the same time, one senses a secret atmosphere, a subtle reality hidden among the surface shapes and colors. The mysteries are obviously represented by the symbols, but they are not directly revealed to the lay person. The one thing that can be perceived is that, under apparently naïve representations, such as the image of the young girl looking at her face in the mirror, lies a great force, the power of mysteries.

However, although a sign and a symbol may be different, the latter can clearly play the part of the former in certain circumstances: the above-mentioned example of

Noah illustrates this reduction of a symbol, or the "freezing" of its meaning, as it has been called.[7] Evidently, both the dove and the olive tree are rich in symbolic meanings: peace, fertility, purity and purification are but a few of these that relate to either of the two; but in Noah's episode, the olive tree and the dove come together to deliver one precise message, or sign, of joy: the land is dry and ready to welcome you and give you its fruits!

---

7. Cf. J. Chevalier, *Dizionario dei simboli*, BUR, Milano, 1989, vol. I, p. XII.

I

THE BIBLE:
THE GREAT BOOK OF SIGNS

Your rod and staff give me courage.

(Ps 23, 4)

For in him we live and move and have our being.

(Acts 17, 28)

1. THE OLD TESTAMENT

I have always felt somewhat envious of the continuous religious meaning that life holds for biblical man. He certainly must interpret reality as something indissolubly linked to God.

If I had to choose, among all the people in the Old Testament, a prototype of the man who sees God at every moment of his existence, I would have a difficult time deciding. Every patriarch, every judge and every prophet of the people of Israel is endowed with the constant vision of God as the Shepherd of life, as Jacob, old and nearing death, refers to the Lord. In the moving blessing of his grandchildren, Ephraim and Manasseh, the aged patriarch seems to encompass in one panoramic view the intricate labyrinths of his adventurous existence, but this overall view is decidedly religious insofar as everything appears to be under God's guidance:

> May the God in whose ways my fathers Abraham and Isaac walked, the God who has been my shepherd from my birth to this day, the Angel who has delivered me from all harm, bless these boys! (Gn 48, 15-16).

The Weeping of the First Minister

Perhaps Joseph inherited from his father this capacity for seeing existence as a whole under God's guidance. At any rate, he is also an axample of one who sees all life as a divine sign. It seems to me that the episode in which his capacity for such a vision culminates is the intensely dramatic scene of his uncontrollable sobbing.

At first, Joseph, who had become accustomed to giving orders, feeling a lump in his throat, had cried out: "Have everyone withdraw from me!" (Gn 45, 1) The doors were closed; the high level of emotional tension was palpable among the servants of the First Minister's chambers, who hurried out. And then everyone heard him.

Zaphenat, vizier of the vast land of Egypt, the Pharaoh's First Minister, who rode in the carriage right behind him, and before whom all bowed low as to a god and reverently shouted *Abrek!*, this deputy Pharaoh was crying. He wept out loud, unashamedly, shedding floods of tears in front of the little group of nomads from the land of Canaan who gazed at him in terror. His behavior made it clear that fear of being judged by others, conventions and etiquette befitting of a high court official all paled and lost their meaning before the undescribable moment he was living:

> His sobs were so loud that the Egyptians heard him (Gn 45, 2).

We will never be able to grasp fully the depth of Joseph's weeping. We tend to see it simply as an emotional outburst on the part of a man whose life has been full of tribulations and rewards. But I think that, while indeed expressing the emotional intensity of the moment, Joseph's tears are the manifestation of an experience that goes well beyond the normal parameters of human emotion. Joseph cries because he sees. As someone who would suddenly behold a tapestry of which until then he had only been able to see the wrong side, Joseph sees, in one exceptional moment, as vividly as can be, the significance and overall splendor of the intricate patterns of his life. He sees his brothers' life also inextricably linked to his, interwoven with his, and he sees it all confirmed from Above. All this happens in a flash, so intense, so unutterable that the only thing he can do is cry in that unique fashion: "His sobs were so loud that the Egyptians heard him".

Zen followers would say that Joseph received an illumination. As a matter of fact, when the emotional intensity seems to subside a little, he speaks to his brothers as if his whole life had indeed been lit up all at once and he wanted to communicate to them this wondrous brightness. Zaphenat forgets his noble Egyptian name and addresses his brothers directly in their ancient mother tongue, the same language they all spoke as children in their father's pastures, and calls himself by his old familiar name:

I am your brother Joseph, whom you once sold into Egypt. But now do not be distressed, do not reproach yourselves for having sold me here. It was really for the sake of saving lives that God sent me here ahead of you. For two years now the famine has been in the land, and for five more years tillage will yield no harvest. God, therefore, sent me on ahead of you to ensure for you a remnant on earth and to save your lives in an extraordinary deliverance. So it was not really you but God who had me come here; and he has made of me a father to Pharaoh, lord of all his household, and ruler over the whole land of Egypt (Gn 45, 4-8).

Thus it is not I nor you, nor any of us who leads, but Someone else. Such is the vision of life passed down to us from the people in the Bible.

God Cast a Stone at Me!

You might think that it is easy to shed tears and to see everything in the divine light when one is second-in-command in the kingdom, surrounded by ministers, and especially when it is others who are struck by misfortune. Instead, the people of Israel hold this spiritual view, handed down by their forefathers, spontaneously and even in the midst of their actual afflictions. As a matter of fact, an insult, a sudden misfortune, a stone cast by the enemy can trigger the vision and the realization that it was Him, God himself who made it happen. For the people in the Bible, the matter is settled.

When David fled Jerusalem, leaving the palace because of his son Absalom's persecution, there must have been considerable turmoil, not only among his followers, but in the entire population who was filled with dismay at the sight of its unhappy king betrayed by his own son. Expressions of anguish and strong emotion abound in the short account of this dramatic event (2Sm 15, 13-23): fear of not being able to escape from Absalom, hurry, distress of the king, and of his faithful supporters, for the unbelievable betrayal, loud crying from the inhabitants of the city as they see their king having to flee on foot. And yet, in the midst of such turmoil, the king's heart never wavers in its profound religious conviction: this moment, as well as David's entire life remains in God's hands. This attidude becomes particularly evident in the episode of Shimei's curse. It is worth rereading to understand what bitter sadness the incident must have caused the king, already deeply wounded:

A man named Shimei came out cursing; he threw stones at David and at all the king's officers, even though all the soldiers, including the royal guard, were on David's right and on his left. Shimei was saying as he cursed: "Away, away, you murderous and wicked man! The Lord has requited you for all the bloodshed in the family of Saul, in whose stead you became king, and the Lord has given over the kingdom to your son Absalom. And now you suffer ruin because you are a murderer"(2 Sm 16, 5-8).

It must be noted that Shimei himself is a biblical man, in other words he too has that same religious sense that "God does everything": it is the Lord who has taken the throne away from David to give it to Absalom. The officers of the king react harshly:

Abishai said to the king: "Why should this dead dog curse my lord the king? Let me go over, please, and lop off his head" (2 Sm 16, 9).

It is at that moment that the king's religious feeling wells up in his heart most clearly and spontaneously: David, as Joseph, *sees God in everything*, and thus, even in his enemy's imprecations, he can read a message from Him who has always been and will always be his shepherd:

"Suppose the Lord has told him to curse David; who then will dare to say: 'Why are you doing this?'" Then the king said to Abishai and all his servants: "If my own son, who came forth from my loins, is seeking my life, how much more might this Benjaminite do so? Let him alone and let him curse, for the Lord has told him to. Perhaps the Lord will look upon my affliction and make it up to me with benefits for the curses he is uttering this day" (2 Sm 16,10-12).

Whenever I read these passages, I envy again the ease with which the biblical people saw God in everything. I think about our enmities, our acts of revenge, petty or serious, our confrontations and misunderstandings with our co-workers, the discord among families and friends... who among us is so limpid, so transparent to God that he can see his mysterious presence in every event, ever provident, and exclaim: "Let my opponent speak, let adversity purify me, for the Lord is present in the midst of it all!".

Job's friends are also surprised at his inability to understand God's continuous language amidst his suffering, since the Lord never ceases to send his messages, even during Job's rest at night:

> For God does speak, perhaps once, or even twice, though one perceive it not.
> In a dream, in a vision of the night, when deep sleep falls upon men, as they slumber in their beds (Jb 33, 14-15).

For the people in the Bible, everything is a sign from God. However, it is possible to state that, apart from its general reading of life in the divine light, the Bible contains the specific "sign" that reveals the presence of God in an even more precise and specific manner.

2. SIGNS IN THE LIVES OF THE PROPHETS

There is a word in the Old Testament that expresses this special sign of the presence of God in life: the Hebrew word *'ot* which is the equivalent of the Greek *semeion*, meaning *sign*. The sign guarantees, as it were, the authenticity of the divine message, for the people as well as for the prophet himself. From Moses to Elijah, from Isaiah to Daniel, to Jesus himself, the emissaries bring with them precious credentials of divine diplomacy: special signs. God spontaneously grants his sign (Is 37, 30) or man asks for it (Is 38,22; 2Kgs 20,8). However, if man is reluctant to recognize the divine message, he will even be invited to request it directly: "Ask for a sign from the Lord, your God", says the prophet to king Ahaz (Is 7, 11).

Small Signs, Great Signs

The signs that accompany the prophet's life are not all of equal significance and impact. Some are extraordinary and miraculous, like the plagues of Egypt and the wonders that Moses performs before the Pharaoh and before the people of Israel during its long journey across the desert; or the spectacular fire which, at Elijah's request, rains down on the stunned prophets of Baal (1Kgs 18, 38).

But other signs are more modest, domestic, as it were. They are drawn from everyday life and they possess the poetic beauty of little things which, under certain circumstances, can also become, simple as they are, emissaries of a spiritual reality. Pots and pans, clothes, belts, tools and so many other objects we use every day come into play; a sudden gesture at a precise moment can turn an event into a prophetic sign: Samuel has just broken off his friendship with Saul, who has rejected God; he is indignant, but as he turns to leave, Saul, who refuses to let him go, seizes a loose end of his mantle, and it tears off. At that moment, Samuel's prophetic intuition awakens and Saul listens in terror to the truth: "The Lord has torn the kingdom of Israel from you this day, and has given it to one who is better than you!" (1Sm 15, 28).

The story of the linen loincloth that God had Jeremiah buy is one of the most beautiful and original episodes (Jer 13, 1-11). The loincloth symbolizes the people of Israel; a whole set of circumstances surrounding it can enlighten whomever meditates on the prophet's significant actions: in the first place, the loincloth is "bought", as slaves are bought, but then it is worn on the loins by the prophet, thereby indicating the closeness of the people to God; later, it is left to rot in a cleft of the rock near the Euphrates. And so the purchase, the hiding place, the humidity, the river, etc. all become signs that must be read within a broader code and that come together to confirm a wider central message: Israel is turning away from God and is losing its identity in the process.

We can meditate on many significant episodes from the lives of the prophets in a similar fashion, episodes such as the tearing by the prophet Ahijah of his new cloak before Jeroboam (1Kgs 11, 29), Jeremiah's visit to the potter's house (Jer 18,1), Ezechiel's drawings on the clay tablet (Ez 4, 1), Zachary's sticks that are named, and so many others.

When Man Becomes a Sign

Often, these signs from everyday life, which seem so simple, so humble, become a real opportunity for the prophet to show unfailing loyalty. This happens especially when the sign has such a profound effect on the life of the prophet that his whole person, sometimes for very long, becomes a sign of God. Hosea is perhaps the most typical and complete example of an entire life elevated to the status of divine sign. His case is also one of the most complex and frequently discussed by biblical exegetes. This mysterious complexity becomes evident from the very beginning of his Book of Prophecies:

> In the beginning of the Lord's speaking to Hosea, the Lord said to Hosea: "Go, take a harlot wife and harlot's children, for the land gives itself to harlotry, turning away from the Lord" (Hos 1,2).

Following this, the prophet's entire life and his personal drama become an intricate web of signs: his children with their symbolic names, his wife's infidelity, the various attempts to get her away from false lovers, her children's accusations, everything can be interpreted in terms of the relationship between God and the people of Israel.

Even if it does not last a lifetime, the sign embodied in the person of the prophet can require time and much hardship before it manifests itself. Thus, the Lord asks Isaiah to go naked and barefoot for three years so that he can tell his people:

> Just as my servant Isaiah has gone naked and barefoot for three years as a sign and portent against Egypt and Ethiopia, so shall the king of Assyria lead away captives from Egypt and exiles from Ethiopia, young and old, naked and barefoot, with buttocks uncovered [the shame of Egypt] (Is 20, 3-4).

From Ezechiel too, God demands a prolonged personal testimony, not without effort and pain: he must lie for days on his right side, then his left one; his food is meager, cooked over human excrement; then comes the silent migration in the darkness (Ez 4, 4-17; 12, 3-20). The prophet can thus accept to be told and pass on to his people the words of the Lord: "I am a sign for you: as I have done, so shall it be done to them" (Ez 12, 11).[1]

3. THE NEW TESTAMENT: JESUS AS THE CENTRAL SIGN

The Great Christian Mandala

I have before my eyes a very beautiful postcard printed in a German abbey.[2] The history of salvation is illustrated in a series of concentric circles at the center of which is Christ Pantocrator. It is like a circular mosaic and very reminiscent of a mandala. If you have seen the miniatures by Beato of Liebana or by the anonymous artist that illustrated on parchment the visions of Saint Hildegarde, you will know what I mean. In the second to last circle, the one closest to the center with Christ, there is a whole company of crowned saints. Some are pointing to the Savior as if to say: "That is the key to the story of salvation, there is the center and the meaning of existence!" It is an icon of exceptional beauty that blends all the colors of the rainbow with the simplicity of primitive art. Green, dark red, sky-blue and orange: the rich hues stand out even more against the gold of so many haloes. But all the colors are only there to enhance the deep blue globe, in the middle of which He appears, the Pantocrator, cloaked in red and gold, seated in the midst of all the worlds with open arms and hands in a regal blessing: the center of centers.

---

1. On the subject of the Old Testament as an eschatological sign, see F. M. Braun, *Jean le Théologien,* vol. II, J. Gabalda Ed., Paris, 1964, pp.189-190.
2. *Allerheiligen*, griechisch, 18. Jh., buch-Kunstverlag Ettal, n.7364.

THE WRITINGS OF:
Maurice Zundel
A genious spiritualist of our century.

THE RELIGION OF LIFE, by Ramon Martinez de Pison Liébanas.
The spirituality of Maurice Zundel
Size 5" x 7 1/2" - 152 pages $ 12.00 US - $ 15.95 CDN

THE INNER PERSON
Maurice Zundel

The reader will find a long meditation, full of new, often unexpected developments. An astonishing and stimulating book, overflowing with richness. After finishing it, the reader will undoubtedly have a better understanding of the essential mystery of his own life: Who am I? And who is God? A retreat preached at the Vatican.

**Size 5" x 7½" – 328 pages
$19.00 US – $24.95 CDN**

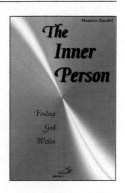

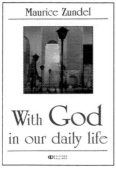

WITH GOD IN OUR DAILY LIFE
Maurice Zundel

Maurice Zundel was a realistic mystic, that is, he was concerned about man in all the dimensions of his personal, social, political and religious life. In this retreat he invites his listeners to live each day and to live each encounter in God's fullness.

**Size 5" x 7½" – 200 pages
$8.00 US – $9.95 CDN**

THE GOSPEL WITHIN
Maurice Zundel

"Never has humanity experienced more tragically the need for God. Most of the time, it seems to reject Him only because it has linked with His name things that are incompatible with the idea that every honest soul is expected to have of Him. We have attempted to show what He is not in order to help our human fellows to develop a sense of what He is." *Maurice Zundel*

**Size 5" x 7½" – 128 pages
$5.50 US – $7.00 CDN**

WONDER AND POVERTY
Maurice Zundel

The goal of this book is to open the way to a profound spiritual experience by subjecting oneself to what Pascal would consider "the order of the heart," where the same mystery is constantly approached in various ways.

Size 5" x 7½" – 176 pages
$7.50 US – $8.95 CDN

ep EDITIONS
PAULINES

ORDER FORM

Quantity	Titre	Price
_____	The Religion of Life	_____
_____	The Inner Person	_____
_____	With God in our Daily Life	_____
_____	The Gospel Within	_____
_____	Wonder and Poverty	_____
_____		Total _____

REMEMBER TO FILL IN YOUR NAME AND ADDRESS BELOW (PRINT OR TYPE)

Name: _____

Address: _____

City: _____ State/Province: _____

Zip/Postal Code: _____ Phone: (_____)_____

Postage and handling charge: $2.50 for one book, plus $1.50 for the second and $0.85 for each additional book.
We do not ship books COD to United States.
Prices subject to change without notice.
Canadian Customers: Please don't forget to add GST (7%) on total amount.

Thank you.

Enclosed amount of $ _____ ☐ Check ☐ Money order

☐ VISA _____ exp. date: _____

☐ MasterCard _____ exp. date: _____

If you are paying with your credit card, the bill will be in Canadian funds.

Mail this order form to:

MÉDIASPAUL

Librairie Médiaspaul
250, rue Saint-François Nord
Sherbrooke (Québec) Canada J1E 2B9
Phone No: (819) 569-5535 / Fax: (819) 565-5474
E-mail: mediaspaul@mediaspaul.qc.ca

Printed in Canada

For me, this postcard visually represents in unequivocal fashion the idea that the whole New Testament is a mandala, the center of which is Christ. The same is true of the old Covenant, but because it is farther away and closer to the surface, it is less obviously exposed to the radiance that emanates from the center, and it does not yet convey the harmony and completeness of the entire mosaic seen as a whole.

About the Christian message, theologians have coined a word which sums up the icon: christocentrism. Ugo of San Vittore speaks of the whole Bible in christocentric terms:

> The Holy Scriptures all speak of Christ and are fulfilled in Christ, because they form one and only book, the book of life which is Christ.[3]

Indeed, from the very first pages of the New Testament, the four evangelists point to Jesus as the great sign foreshadowed for centuries in the prophecies and in the preceding cycles of the history of salvation; and so they often use the phrase "as it is written", thus indicating that the old Scriptures are being fulfilled in the words, the deeds and the whole person of Jesus. The three synoptic gospels, as well as John's, begin their stories along those lines. In this regard, it is interesting to study and compare the content of the first chapter in each of the four gospels.

---

3. *De arca Noe morali*, 11, 8-9.

The First Signs in the Evangelical Account

Matthew presents Jesus's genealogy as evidence of his Isrealite ancestry and of his being the depository of the messianic promises. Immediately after, he gives the account of his miraculous birth and proceeds to show concretely how this event corresponds to what the prophets had foretold. He uses words similar to the ones just mentioned, which he often repeats throughout his gospel:

> All this took place to fulfill what the Lord had said through the prophet:"Behold, the virgin shall be with child and bear a son, and they shall name him Emmanuel" (Mt 1,22-23).

Mark begins in the same way:

> As it is written in Isaiah the prophet: "Behold, I am sending my messenger ahead of you; he will prepare your way..." John the Baptist appeared in the desert proclaiming a baptism of repentance... (Mk 1, 2-4).

Later he shows how these things were accomplished: Jesus comes to the river Jordan and his coming is accompanied by extraordinary signs that substantiate his being the beloved Son of God (Mk 1, 9-11).

Luke begins his book of "careful research" by giving a more profuse and detailed account of the miraculous events leading up to the birth of Jesus, such as Zechariah's encounter with the angel Gabriel during the liturgical service in the Temple, which is already a double sign: for Zechariah himself, who becomes mute for not having immediately believed the angel's words, as well as for the people who, surprised by Zechariah's unusual hesitation before the "Holy of Holies", can soon bear out his dumbness that prevents him from giving the customary ritual blessing before the congregation (Lk 1, 5-22).

John, the evangelist of "signs" par excellence, proclaims Jesus as Messiah and Son of God from the signs that confirm his mission. After his magnificent Prologue in which he calls Christ the "light that shines in the darkness" (Jn 1, 5), he begins the account of the first *semeia* or significant events, signs of light, through which whoever can see will understand that God the Father lives and operates in his Son Jesus.

The Light from the Signs of Jesus

Jesus's entire life is suffused with this continuous, extraordinary, mysterious confirmation of his identity: the light from the signs. His birth is surrounded by significant events: the angels announce it through dreams and visions; in the Far East, a mysterous star catches the eye of a group of scholars and leads them to Herod's court, causing the king of Judea to undertake a search with his advisers's assistance. But in the midst of these miraculous events already emerges the "humble sign", typical of Jesus' messianic language: from the moment he enters history, he does not claim to dazzle and convince against all odds, nor to prove beyond any doubt that he is the Messiah, but rather he leaves the door open to meditation and to freely-chosen personal growth in those who wish to receive the signs. The role of the "humble sign", the "little brother sign", is to counterbalance the effect of the more grandiose and dazzling ones. And so, the royal child revealed by the star is born of a poor family, and he will not be found, as might be expected, in Herod's palace, but in a much more modest place, a manger. As a matter of fact, the child will be persecuted and sought by the authorities as an obstacle and a threat to the power of the king. In the final analysis, small and great signs are united in one message and always point to Him, immensely great and infinitely humble at the same time, resplendent and obscure, well-known and forgotten, as living invitations to enquiry and meditation to all men of good will. It is the angels who deliver this wonderful key message to the poor, frightened shepherds; the words they hear sum up what is the constant combination of light and shadow of the messianic manifestation of Christ:

> For today in the city of David
> a savior
> has been born for you
> who is Messiah the Lord.
> And this will be a sign for you:
> you will find an infant
> wrapped in swaddling clothes
> and lying in a manger (Lk 2, 11-12).

I have divided this dense key message in many short phrases, so that everyone can meditate on them and discover the marvellous wealth and depth of meaning of the language, the same which is also typical of the teachings of Jesus who, whether by word or deed, always strives to awaken consciences to the truth. Each word, each phrase is a magnificent revelation. Indeed, whoever shall meditate on them, and whose intuition will unveil the mystery they conceal, will experience great joy (cf. Lk 2, 10).

To this language of signs connected to the birth of Jesus one can add the words spoken by the elder Simeon at the infant's Presentation in the Temple. Walking away from the groups of people that fill the various halls of the Temple, just milling around or seeking spiritual enlightenment from the rabbis, Simeon takes the child into his trembling arms and, lifting him, says:

> "Behold, this child is destined for the fall and rise of many in Israel, and to be a sign that will be contradicted so that the thoughts of many hearts may be revealed" (Lk 2, 34-35).

For the second time in Luke's gospel, the person of the newborn himself is presented as a sign: a humble and joyful sign for the shepherds, a sign of contradiction for many generations to come.

The Signs in Jesus' Public Life

Once Jesus leaves Galilee to embark on his public ministry by first retiring into the desert for forty days, all around him emerges again the language of signs that surrounds his childhood, with its typical pattern of light and shadow. It will remain the way in which Christ manifests himself up until his Crucifixion and Resurrection.

The silent time spent in the desert already displays the characteristic multiple meanings that illuminate Christ's work and reveal deeper layers in the sense of his mission. In the first place, the number forty is itself significant. It appears in many biblical texts in reference to the seclusion in the desert. Moses himself spent forty days and forty nights on Mount Sinai without bread or water (Ex 24, 18), and Elijah walked forty days and forty nights to mount Horeb (1Kg 19, 8). Moreover, Moses and Elijah are the very same prophets who appear with Jesus on mount Tabor during his Transfiguration. On this third sacred mountain and in the person of Jesus, they encounter the mysterious presence of Yahweh they had met on Sinai and on Horeb, after days of solitude and fasting.

As the stay in the desert is drawing to a close, another episode takes place, typical of the language of messianic signs that surround Jesus: the temptations. In these, Jesus decisevely rejects one particular style of self-manifestation and embraces another. What he rejects is the spectacular messianic demonstration suggested by the Temptor: if he is truly the Son of God, let him prove it to all with a powerful and irrefutable sign, let him throw himself from the parapet of the temple, only to fall softly from the sky, since the angels will surely rush to support him as the bewildered crowd of temple worshipers looks on. Leaving aside an exegetic examination of how the temptations occured concretely, it is nonetheless certain that Jesus' refusal has a very clear meaning: he has no wish to reveal himself to mankind in any manner other than that decreed by God's plan. In my opinion, the fact that Jesus rejects the spectacular sign to embrace the humble one has been overemphasized. I do not believe that he absolutely rejects the extraordinary, supernatural sign in itself, but rather the seeking of one's glory through certain signs independently of God's design. And that is how his refusal must be interpreted: "One does not live by bread alone, but by every word that comes forth from the mouth of God" (Mt 4, 3-4), "You shall not put the Lord, your God, to the test" (4, 7), "The Lord, your God shall you worship and him alone shall you serve" (4,10). Throughout Christ's public life, extraordinary, supernatural signs do indeed appear, signs that alter the normal course of events and astound the crowd: the raising of Lazarus from the dead, the multiplication of the loaves of bread, the calming of the storm and the walking on water. These signs are not so different from those suggested by the Temptor in the desert. The difference lies in the fact that the extraordinary signs that accompany Jesus at specific moments of his life are always in harmony with the Father's will and with the typical style of messianic revelation hich the Father has chosen for his Son, a style that also includes obscurity, persecution, suffering and death.

John's gospel, which some scholars actually refer to as the "gospel of signs", is particularly suited to the study and meditation of this style of semiological language that characterizes Christ's public ministry. Every miraculous sign in this gospel is a magnificent apocalypse on the person of Jesus, as well as an invitation to believe in him addressed to those who feel ready to awaken and open their eyes to the profound meaning of the events they are told. After the miracles, Jesus himself provides an explanation that elevates them from the level of merely amazing occurences to that of significant events on a spiritual and divine plane. For instance, the multiplication of the loaves is followed by the words: "I am the bread of life" (Jn 6, 48), the healing of the man blind from birth is preceded by: "While I am in the world, I am the light of the world" (Jn 9, 5), and the raising of Lazarus by: "I am the resurrection and the life" (Jn 11, 25).

The first conclusion of John's gospel contains these words that sum up the meaning of the continuous language of messianic signs:

> Now Jesus did many other signs in the presence of his disciples that are not written in this book. But these are written that you may believe that Jesus is the Messiah, the Son of God, and that through this belief you may have life in his name (Jn 20, 30-31).

4. JESUS, MASTER OF SIGNS

Jesus is often called rabbi. Rabbis were completely devoted to God and the study of his law, the *Torah*. They were the "masters" par excellence who taught the wisdom of the Holy Scriptures to their disciples crouching at their feet. Deeply religious, they were considered as men of God and revered as such by the people; many of them have gone down in history as spiritual guides of the Hebrew people, responsible for its religion. Hillel and Sammai were Christ's contemporaries; both almost mythical figures in the teaching of the *Torah*, they died before the time of Christ's public life; Gamaliel, Hillel's nephew, and his opponent, Iokanan ben Zakkai, taught when Jesus was going to the temple; the very young rabbi Joshua used to teach on the mountain near lake Tiberiad.

In this context, Jesus is called "rabbi", not only by his own disciples, but by the very authoritative rabbis who approach him. This is not the place to carefully examine Jesus' teaching in comparison to that of the rabbis; there were undoubtedly some differences in both method and attitude, which were readily noticed by the people who listened, filled with wonder, to the parables and sayings of the master from Galilee. I would like to dwell on one aspect of his teaching which I call "spiritual discernment", that is, the art of reading the signs of God.

The Teaching of Discernment Through Questions

If we understand that Jesus presents himself as a sign, it is obvious that his teaching on discernment focuses on opening the eyes of his disciples, and then of the people, to the true significance of his mission and his work.

Typically, discernment is awakened by asking questions. This method was often used by rabbis to bring about in their disciples the awareness of the profound meaning of the law. Jesus too would very often question his disciples about his person and the meaning of his miracles: "Who do people say that the Son of Man is?... But who do you say that I am?" (Mt 16, 13-15). Just as any teacher likes to arouse his pupils' interest with interrogative exclamations and is surprised by how slowly they learn, Jesus the master tries to make his disciples understand the true meaning of the miraculous signs and is struck by their inability to grasp it: "Do you not yet understand, and do you not remember the five loaves for the five thousand, and how many wicker baskets you took up?" (Mt 16,9). The passage that parallels this one in Mark is especially beautiful in this regard, as it is marked by the candor of the questions and answers one expects in a compulsory school situation:

> "Do you not yet understand or comprehend? Are your hearts hardened? Do you have eyes and not see, ears and not hear? And do you not remember, when I broke the five loaves for the five thousand, how many wicker baskets full of fragments you picked up".
> "Twelve".
> "When I broke the seven loaves for the four thousand, how many full baskets of fragments did you pick up?"
> "Seven".
> "Do you still not understand?" (Mk 8, 17-21).[4]

---

4. I have omitted on purpose the inserted "They answered him", "He said to them", etc. to bring out the liveliness of this exchange.

However, Jesus does not limit himself to asking questions about past miracles. He questions the disciples on the very scene of the miracle, immediately before or right after it is performed. Completely in command of the situation, Jesus sees right through the scribes, who are shocked because they heard him forgive the sins of a paralytic, and he asks them:

> "Why are you thinking such things in your hearts? Which is easier, to say to the paralytic, 'Your sins are forgiven', or to say, 'Rise, pick up your mat and walk'?
> But that you may know that the Son of Man has authority to forgive sins on earth, I say to you—he said to the paralytic—rise, pick up your mat and go home." He rose, picked up his mat at once, and went away in the sight of everyone (Mk 2, 8-12).

This is one of the clearest passages in the gospel to understand the teaching of Jesus on signs. There is no doubt that the scribes who witness the scene know that the power to forgive belongs only to God: "Who but God alone can forgive sins?" It is important to grasp the words "God alone" in their strongest sense to perceive the intensity of the moment and the full impact of the subsequent sign. Jesus immediately raises everything to another plane: the plane of He who alone can forgive sins. His miracle thus means: "If God alone can forgive, then you understand from this sign who is the one who stands among you with the power to forgive".

Still very much in command, but in front of a much simpler audience—maybe only Peter and the collectors of the temple tax—Jesus asks Peter: "What is your opinion, Simon? From whom do the kings of the earth take tolls of census tax? From their subjects[5] or from foreigners?" (Mt 17, 25). Once again, the question from the Master of signs prepares the way for the elevation of the heart to the spiritual plane. This time, Jesus will use the great symbol of the Temple of God to open the eyes of his audience.

The Temple! "There is but one temple for the one and only God" was the principal emotion that stirred within any true child of Israel at the sight of that mighty symbol. The holiest place in the city aroused boundless admiration and devotion in the hearts of the Hebrews. Still today, they pray and weep before the vestiges of that sacred place, the Wailing Wall. As they gazed at the glistening marble building and its golden spires blazing in the Judean sun, the pilgrims who came to Jerusalem every year to celebrate Passover could still hear, echoing deep down, the words of young king Salomon, spoken at the inauguration of the first Temple: "Can it indeed be that God dwells among men on earth? If the heavens and the highest heavens cannot contain you, how much less this temple which I have built!... May your eyes watch night and day over this temple, the place where you have decreed you shall be honored" (1 Kgs 8, 27-29).

It is therefore imperative to understand the significance of the symbol "temple" in the context of the sign that Jesus is about to reveal. Every adult male Jew was obliged to make a contribution to the upkeep of the dwelling of the Almighty. Peter's answer to Jesus' questions is immediately followed by a confirmation from the Master when he says, again to spark an intuition in Peter himself and in his

---

5. The Greek word translated here as *subjects* literally means "sons".

other listeners: "Then the subjects (sons) are exempt." And then comes this peaceful and extraordinary reaffirmation of a very special sign:

> "But that we may not offend them, go to the sea, drop in a hook and take the first fish that comes up. Open its mouth and you will find a coin worth twice the temple tax. Give that to them for me and for you." (Mt 17, 27).

The Son does not want to offend those whose eyes have not yet been opened, but he gives a sign to all, the meaning of which is easily grasped: he is the true Son of He who dwells in the Holy of Holies and who is also master of all tributes.

The Signs in the Language of Jesus

Beyond the question and the confirmation of his teaching through signs provided "on the spot", Jesus uses in his preaching an entire symbolic language in which the humble sign, the little brother sign, constantly appears.

Simple flashes of everyday life are a means to convey the loftiest spiritual realities. The process is always the same: a change of level, or the opening of the inner eye and its turning to a higher plane. This way, a simple coin, a patch, a fishing net, yeast, sheep in a meadow, the money paid to lowly workers, a nursery rhyme sung by children playing in the town square, all these things are signs, our ever-present little brothers, simple and familiar, yet given prominence and depth in the Master's words by the fact that they become messengers of the kingdom of heaven.

The Teaching of Discernment
Through the Signs of Nature

Beside household implements and daily chores, Jesus also uses the world of nature to open the minds of his disciples to the reading of signs. Taking as an example the ease with which most people know how to interpret the signs in nature, Jesus at times urges his disciples to look up to a higher plane even more directly than in the parables:

"In the evening you say: 'Tomorrow will be fair, for the sky is red'; and in the morning: 'Today will be stormy, for the sky is red and threatening'. You know how to judge the appearance of the sky, but you cannot judge the signs of the times?" (Mt 16, 2-3).

When he teaches through images drawn from nature, Jesus occasionally adds an extraordinary sign to confirm his words, as in the case of the bare fig tree that withers after he speaks, to the disciples' amazement (Mt 21, 18-22). The fig tree becomes the sign with which Jesus teaches the power of faith or—on a more subtle plane—the blindness and lack of belief of the hardened people of Israel.

Perhaps the finest example of Jesus' teaching through the signs of nature is his invitation to look at the birds and the lilies of the fields as windows opening up our awareness to God's continuous providence (Mt 6, 25-34). This point will be examined more closely in the second part of the book.

There is one aspect of Jesus' language relating to the signs of nature that has always struck me and, although at first glance it may seem out of context, it must not be overlooked. In the middle of an eschatological discourse, as he foretells the cosmic catastrophes that will precede the glorious coming of the Son of Man at the end of time, Christ uses a little brother sign, infinitely delicate and extraordinarly beautiful, all the more so as it appears next to mighty and terrifying images:

> "Consider the fig tree and all the other trees. When their buds burst open, you see for yourselves and know that summer is now near; in the same way, when you see these things happening, know that the kingdom of God is near" (Lk 21, 29-33).

Next to the signs of the sun and the moon, of all the heavenly bodies overturned, of the roaring sea and lashing waves and of people dying of fright in anticipation of what is coming upon the world, the sign of the fig tree forms a sharp contrast, with poetic overtones. In this passage of his dense and mysterious eschatological teachings, Christ tells us that those events that will cause anguish and death to so many will be something altogether different for those who will have learned to *see the signs* with a transparent heart. For them, the very same signs will carry the meaning and scent of spring!

The Two Basic Principles of Discernment

Two great principles form the basis for Jesus' teaching on signs. The first one, also taken from the imagery of nature, is the link between the tree and its fruit:

> "Either declare the tree good and its fruit is good, or declare the tree rotten and its fruit is rotten, for a tree is known by its fruit" (Mt 12, 33).

This simple principle will help us to unmask false prophets (Mt 7, 15-20), to judge the hearts of men (Mt 15, 10-20) and not to be confused by the doctrine of the Pharisees and the Sadducees (Mt 16, 5-12); generally speaking, it is the pivot on which hinges the Christian tradition on spiritual discernment.

The second principle, closer to the Oriental practices well known in the West, is the principle of constant awareness and transparency: "Awake! Be watchful!" are words often spoken by Christ to draw his disciples' attention to the language of signs, such as his invitation to awaken before the beauty of the lilies: "Observe, look, do not spend your life in a slumber!". This second principle, referred to by some as the virtue of Christian vigilance, finds its most beautiful expression in the passage in which Jesus speaks of his return and of the need to always be awake and watchful to know the moment of his coming (Lk 12, 35-40). He uses a most striking image: every time I recall it, I have spontaneous flashes on the world of silent meditation. It is a call to continuous meditation itself, that is, to constant awareness, which is like a lamp perpetually lit in our lives. The passage even alludes to the typical stance of one who is ready and in control:

> "Gird your loins and light your lamps and be like servants who await their master's return from a wedding, ready to open immediately when he comes and knocks. Blessed are those servants whom the master finds vigilant on his arrival. Amen, I say to you, he will gird himself, have them recline at the table, and proceed to wait on them. And should he come on the second or third watch and find them prepared in this way, blessed are those servants."

The Effects of Jesus' Teaching

The results produced by these teachings on the listeners were neither uniform nor definitive. Following Jesus' own principles, we can distinguish three categories of people to examine the effects of his teaching or of the signs he gave in order to corroborate his word.

First, there are the hard-hearted, who are reluctant to see. Not only do they remain closed to the teaching, but they overtly oppose the Master's words and evade the significance of miracles. Their imperviousness is described in a text by the prophet Isaiah which Jesus himself quotes in order to confirm how difficult it is for one who is closed and hard-hearted to understand the language of signs:

> You shall indeed hear but not understand,
> you shall indeed look but never see.
> Gross is the heart of these people,
> they will hardly hear with their ears,
> they have closed their eyes,
> lest they see with their eyes
> and hear with their ears
> and understand with their heart and be converted
> and I heal them (Mt 13, 14-15).

Then there are those who initiate an opening to the reading of signs and to the true meaning of Jesus' words, without evasion. They allow themselves to be overcome by the mysterious power of his teaching and by its amazing confirmation in the signs that follow. Such is the case of the Samaritan woman; struck by the prophetic force of Jesus' words, she says to the townspeople: "Come see a man who has told me everything I have done. Could he possibly be the Messiah?" (Jn 4, 29). We can see the same early stages of openness in the interest shown by Nicodemus, who approaches Jesus at night, perhaps fearful of doing so in broad daylight, but who is positively struck by the signs done by the Master and eager to better understand their meaning. Besides, being a Pharisee and scholar of the Scriptures, Nicodemus does not fail to recognize in Jesus the traits of a true rabbi, and maybe he speaks on behalf of a group of sympathizers like himself: "Rabbi, we know that you are a teacher who has come from God, for no one can do these signs that you are doing unless God is with him" (Jn 3, 2).

We find a third group of people who open completely to Jesus' teaching and fully understand the meaning of his signs. They are the opposite of those in the first group and described as such immediately after the text quoted above:

> "But blessed are your eyes, because they see, and your ears, because they hear. Amen, I say to you, many prophets and righteous people longed to see what you see but did not see it, and to hear what you hear but did not hear it" (Mt 13, 16-17).

This group *knows how to see* and fulfills to perfection the principle inherent to any true discernment: to be vigilant, to keep one's eyes open to see the sign and to have a transparent heart in order to understand it. Whoever is familiar with the gospels will clearly see that the main representatives of this category are the disciples. However, we must not think that discernment happens all of a sudden. As in any human teaching, the Master probably had to overcome in his disciples a certain laziness and initial incredulity. We have already noted that Jesus reprimanded his disciples for their lack of faith.

Peter as an Example

Peter is an interesting example of the varying degrees of openness in a heart that is drawn to Jesus, but is not yet sufficiently limpid and pure to understand the full import of the Master's signs. Indeed, with characteristic enthusiasm, Peter is fascinated by the first extraordinary sign received from Christ: the miraculous catch of fish. Overcome by intense emotion in the face of Jesus' purity and, at the same time, perfectly aware of the impurity of his own heart, he falls to his knees before Jesus on the sandy shore and says: "Depart from me, Lord, for I am a sinful man!" (Lk 5, 8). The same impetuous reaction prompts him to ask Jesus to make him walk on the waves, like him, and this he asks as a sign to confirm his faith in Jesus, who is sent by God. The scene that follows, in which Peter, urged by Jesus, earnestly throws himself in the sea, and his doubts that lead to his beginning to sink, are also a beautiful example of a faith and a heart not yet mature (Mt 14, 22-23).

Peter's growth in the art of *knowing how to see the signs* becomes manifest especially in regard to the person of Jesus, himself a sign. Peter will be indeed the first to receive the enlightenment from the Father, which will enable him to openly confess Christ the Messiah and Son of the Living God (Mt 16, 13-19). And again, at a time of crisis in Capernaum, when belief in Jesus is in doubt, and many of the disciples pull back and even leave the Master, it is Peter who dares to speak on behalf of the small group of Twelve to confirm that they fully adhere to his person and teaching. It is nice to detect in his words the sincere intuition that springs from the heart of the coarse fisherman from Galilee; even though he may not yet know how to express himself well, Peter is clearly becoming increasingly open, receptive:

> Jesus then said to the Twelve: "Do you also want to leave?" Simon Peter answered him: "Master, to whom shall we go? You have the words of eternal life. We have come to believe and are convinced that you are the Holy One of God" (Jn 6, 67-69).

The openness and transparency of Peter's heart reach their fullness in Pentecost. As he addresses the crowd, surrounded by the remaining ten disciples, his words are also an affirmation that Jesus' teaching on signs has borne fruit and has made its way into the heart of the Galilean fisherman:

> "You who are Israelites, hear these words. Jesus the Naz-arean was a man commended to you by God with mighty deeds, wonders and signs, which God worked through him in your midst, as you yourselves know. This man, delivered up by the set plan and foreknowledge of God, you killed, using lawless men to crucify him... God raised this Jesus; of this, we are all witnesses" (Acts 2, 22-23, 32).

Peter not only shows that he can read simply and clearly the signs that confirm the messianic nature of Jesus and illuminate the history of Israel, but the effect created on his audience shows that he has also received the gift of penetrating men's hearts in order to initiate them to the art of *knowing how to see*:

> Now, when they heard this, they were cut to the heart, and they asked Peter and the other apostles: "What are we to do, my brothers?" (Acts 2, 37).

Jesus' teaching on how to discern and read the signs of God in life is carried on in the church through his disciples. The list of signs confirming the presence of God's Spirit is well known; the text in which Paul describes them to the Galatians as the opposite of the signs of the "flesh", that is, of the world, is a classic in any study on spiritual discernment (Gal 5, 19-33). Christ himself already announces to the disciples, at the end of Mark's gospel, a series of signs and wonders that will accompany their preaching, thus manifesting the truth of the gospel (Mk 16, 17-20). It is also in this sense that Paul says to the Corinthians: "The signs of an apostle were performed among you" (2 Cor 12,12).

5. THE SIGN OF JONAH

The great sign with which God definitively commends the person of Jesus as the Messiah is his death and resurrection. Jesus himself, on several occasions, proclaims this event as a definitive sign, and he does so through various images, as the image of the temple rebuilt in three days, or more directly, speaking of his own death and of his rising on the third day. But of all the metaphors of resurrection used by Jesus, the one that seems to me to be the most profound is the one of the prophet Jonah to whom he compares himself:

> Then some of the scribes and Pharisees said to him: "Teacher, we wish to see a sign from you." He said to them in reply: "An evil and unfaithful generation seeks a sign, but no sign will be given it, except the sign of Jonah the prophet. Just as Jonah was in the belly of the whale three days and three nights, so will the Son of Man be in the heart of the

earth three days and three nights. At the judgment, the men of Niniveh will arise with this generation and condemn it, because they repented at the preaching of Jonah; and there is something greater than Jonah here. At the judgment, the queen of the south will arise with this generation and condemn it, because she came from the ends of the earth to hear the wisdom of Solomon; and there is something greater than Solomon here" (Mt 12, 38-42).

This text, enigmatic and disputed by many exegetes, is rich in meanings that illuminate the last and greatest sign in the life of Jesus.

The Context of the Sign of Jonah

The sign of Jonah is given by Jesus in a powerfully dramatic moment. Indeed, it arises in the midst of a controversial comparison between antagonistic plans and expectations. There is tension created by a lack of faith and the aprioristic refusal of the person of Jesus, in spite of the miraculous signs performed by him and known to all: the Pharisees ask for yet another definitive sign. Perhaps what they insisted for was a rabbinical type of sign, as has been hypothesized, that is to say a sign that would occur at a pre-established time and place, possibly of a meteorological nature.

What we see here once more is the typical language of the world, which demands obvious demonstrations, in its own way, with conditions according to its own specifications: "As we want, not as you want." And we also notice the similarity of this type of requirement with the messianic manifestations suggested by the Temptor to Jesus, at the beginning of his public life. What characterizes the sign in worldly terms is always the same thing: its being outside God's plan, lack of faith or an agnostic view in regard to a possible divine design; instead, one independently and selfishly chooses one's own plan.

Jesus grieves over this, he gets angry. Mark tells us that he heaved a deep sigh and said: "Why does this generation ask for a sign?" (8, 12). Matthew and Luke add to the expression "this generation" adjectives that clearly indicate the level of tension and Jesus' indignation (considering all the obvious signs already given!): "An evil and unfaithful generation seeks a sign" (Mt 12, 39); "This generation is an evil generation" (Lk 11, 29).

After these introductory remarks, the terms are reversed: "Not as you will, but as the Father wills it in his design", and then the great design is announced with details of time and space: "No sign will be given [to this generation] except the sign of Jonah the prophet. Just as Jonah was in the belly of the whale three days and three nights, so will be the Son of Man be in the heart of the earth three days and three nights" (Mt 12, 39-40).

Jesus offers the sum total of his person and of his life as a sign: his life, his preaching supported by miracles, his death and resurrection are compared to the person and mission of Jonah the prophet (cf. Jn 2, 1). Just as Jonah was sent by God as a sign of salvation to the people of Niniveh so that it would convert, and just as he stayed in the belly of the whale three days and three nights, so was Jesus sent to an even more incredulous people, and so will it unfold as regards the definitive sign of his death and resurrection on the third day.

The sign of Jonah, the great and definitive sign of the coming of the Son of God among us, is also accompanied by other small clues that Jesus intersperses here and there, as the moment of his death is approaching: the brief allusion to the grain of wheat, that also lies in the depths of the earth, only to come out with new fruit-bearing life (Jn 12, 24); the mysterious words at the Last Supper: "I will not leave you orphans; I will come to you. In a little while, the world will no longer see me, but you will see me" (Jn 14, 18-19); "A little while and you will no longer see me, and again a little while later and you will see me" (Jn 16, 16).

The Empty Tomb Concludes the Sign of Jonah

The last key to the sign of Jonah is the empty tomb on the third day after Jesus' death. The empty tomb is the last clue and the last opportunity for the typical messianic language of signs to come to its conclusion. For those who have opened their eyes and ears to the message of Jesus, it is an initiation to a new life but, at the same time, it is a condemnation for the hard-hearted.

The empty tomb is both a sign of contradiction and evidence for those who come near it, as did happen on the morning of the resurrection. Two groups of people had the chance to understand the sign of Jonah. The first group is represented by believers, and its prototype is John, the young disciple who, on seeing the empty tomb, understands everything in a flash:

Then the other disciple also went in, the one who had arrived at the tomb first, and he saw and believed (Jn 20, 8).

The other group, represented by the hard-hearted, reacts in a diametrically opposed fashion before the empty tomb:

They assembled with the elders and took counsel; then they gave a large sum of money to the soldiers, telling them: "You are to say, 'His disciples came by night and stole him while we were asleep.' And if this gets to the ears of the governor, we will satisfy him and keep you out of trouble" (Mt 28, 12-14).

Such schemers, whose language is all about money, power and lies, Christ refers to with one word: the "world", leaving them, blind, in the house of the dead:

"In a little while, the world will no longer see me, but you will see me, because I live and you will live" (Jn 14, 19).

* * *

The Finger Pointing to the Moon

A well-known image in the Zen tradition is a finger pointing to the moon. I believe that, as a whole, the Bible, the great book of signs, is like a mysterious divine finger, or rather many fingers, all pointing to the moon. On the last page of the last book of the Scriptures, Revelation—the book that more than any other in the Old or New Testament speaks to us through signs—, on this page that puts the last seal on the entire revelation, is unveiled the point of light toward which aim all the pages of the Bible:

"I, Jesus, sent my angel to give you this testimony for the churches. I am the root and offspring of David, the bright morning star" (Rv 22, 16).

That is the mighty star to which points the finger of the great book of signs. The whole purpose of the Bible is none other than to point to the bright morning star. Woe to us if we overturn this beautiful image and become more interested in the finger than in the star; we would then be like children, incapable of leaving their cradle, sucking their finger, absorbed in self-worship! But the finger is doubtless needed to help us look up and notice the star, the alpha and omega of the Bible, and, having found our bearings, to walk toward its spendor. Thus the Holy Scriptures are our letter of awakening; in so many ways, through different literary genres, images, parables and signs, the Bible repeats, over and over, the refrain of an ancient Christian hymn:

Awake, O sleeper,
and arise from the dead,
and Christ will give you light (Eph 5, 14).

II

THE SIGNS IN NATURE

In paradise, where every twig
sings the name of God,
a rose does not spread its perfume:
it spreads the Name of God.

YÛNUS EMRE

1. THE OTHER BIBLE

"The heavens tell of the glory of God...".

It was announced in the first Bible: there is a second Bible that sends special messages from God to mankind. Special because they are not expressed in written words, as in the first Bible: "It is not a language, they are not words".[1] Special messages nonetheless that can be found all over the earth, but having nothing to do with the written word.

The signs in nature, the second Bible, can be perceived by all; however, only those with simple hearts are naturally open to this type of perception from ordinary life. Mystics and poets also generally possess enough simplicity and limpidity to tune in on the special wave length that runs through the whole of creation. Siddharta, the well-known seeker in Herman Hesse's novel by the same name, understands beautifully the language of the river, but only at the end of his spiritual quest, whereas Vasudeva, the old, simple ferryman, has always listened to it and understood its message:

> "Is it not true, old friend, that the river has many voices, many, many voices? Does it not have the voice of a king, and that of a warrior, and that of a bull, of a night bird, and of a woman in labor, and of someone moaning, and a thousand other voices?"
> "So it is—admitted Vasudeva—: the voices of all creatures are within its own."

---

1. I prefer this version, in the Jerusalem Bible, of verse 4 of Psalm 19: "There is no word or sound; no voice is heard", alluding to the stars as "the silent writing in the heavens".

The Joy of God in Creation

It would be impossible to include in this book even a minute part of the immense riches and wisdom contained in the messages of nature. We shall deal with only a few in a brief essay whose goal is to initiate and encourage to the reading of this second Bible in its entirety. You will see that all the signs in nature loudly proclaim to mankind its communion in the joy and bliss of the Creator Himself. After all, paradise, as an archetype of man's innermost self, has been portrayed from the most remote times as a vast, joyful garden, which is an expression of the ecstasy of creation. A blade of grass as well as the infinite starry vault can lead to this ecstasy. Francis of Assisi, John of the Cross and so many other saints and poets speak in simple terms of the hymn of joy that rises from the thousand voices of the sun, the moon, the waves, mountains and islands. Mystics from the Orient even speak of "the music of heavenly bodies", which is reminiscent of the stars that, rejoycing in unison, "sang in chorus" (Jb 38, 7), and of the "silent music" in the *Spitual Canticle* by John of the Cross (Stanza 15).

We find that joy always underlies these phrases, a healthy, transparent joy, at times similar to that of young children at play, skipping and running through the meadows. A contemporary writer describes creation as a perpetual game that God plays to make human beings glad. In this vision of creation, man is like a child who, fascinated and excited by the game, asks his father with straigh-forward insistence: "Again, do it again!"

That is the first sign of the second Bible: God is laughing in nature, he is having fun; he is playing with us and, again and again, he repeats for us the miracle of the sun and the stars, the kaleidoscope of colors in plants, the thousand rhythms of the dance of seasons, the melody of every breath of wind, the glorious song of every bird in the world who greets the new light of day. Because God knows that the inner child in every man—even though he may not be willing to admit it—loves to play and cannot do without this exhilarating daily game of the signs of creation. And so man will always ask for its wonder, using a secret language, without words, that filial language that only an experienced parent can understand and translate as: "Once more, please, do it again!"

2. THE SACRED, WATCHFUL TREES

I do not quite know how to tell you without sounding rhetorical, or poetic, or what not... Most of all, I fear I might not treat them with all the respect and reverence they deserve: trees!

It was many years ago, while reading Thomas Merton's works, that I suddenly grasped the holiness of trees. Trees are holy, I was able to ascertain it many times in my life.

If, as Saint Ireneus says, God's glory is a living man, God's glory is also a living tree, all the more so if one considers how some human beings can hardly be said to be God's glory.

Standing before any tree, you will find yourself before a mystery of holiness. The most humble of trees, covered with dust and weakened by pollution in a dreary city yard, yet keeping us company and alleviating our insane collective asphyxiation by offering a little green, is also a precious sign of holiness. A tree comes extraordinarily close to God because, without distorsions, with total ingenuousness and authenticity, it simply fulfills the mission for which it was put on this planet. It imitates the creative concept that God has of himself; it bears within itself something of God's own depths. Unlike man, a tree will never attempt to be other than it is. That is why it can communicate its message of holiness without hindrance, from the time it starts growing from seed to the day it dies. I too thus hear the message "gloria Dei arbor vivens". Much more, even "arbor moriens" is a splendid message that glorifies the Creator.

The Dead Tree in Zaïre

I shall never forget it. Generally speaking, the roads that link big cities through the vastness of Central Africa are clear and straight. But on that day, the road from Kikwit to Kinshasa was blocked. A long line of stopped cars forced us to get out of our vehicle to investigate the cause of this unusual traffic jam. It was simply the death of a tree. There it was, huge, like its African brothers, imposing enough to stop traffic in the middle of the bush even more dramatically than a policeman in the city. It lay there in front of everybody, and its heavy and sturdy trunk had an air of silent dignity and elegance about it, in sharp contrast with the insignificant little people shouting and bustling all around it, quite powerless in the face of this strange, gigantic corpse, whose death was most troublesome and inopportune.

At that point, the two cultures, the African and the European, came to the surface, each revealing itself in the presence of the tree. There was some sort of spontaneous funeral, a ritual which I have never forgotten and shall remember as long as I live. Without really being aware of what they were doing, each of the two cultures paid its particular brand of last respects. The Africans, who were closer to the tree, were dancing. They did so naturally, expressing their feelings through rhythm, in a fashion typical of every celebration and sacred event in the life of African communities. Their reaction clearly showed that this event, which at first appeared to be an unforseen, unsurmountable problem, had now become dance, a spontaneous manifestation of one of the greatest gifts that God gave this wonderful people: the ability to transform life into poetry, rhythm and song.

We, the Europeans, also hastened to pay tribute to the tree in our own peculiar way. We were going up and down the line of cars, consulting one another on how to deal with the problem in the fastest, most efficient way. Somebody pulled out a chain saw. Very soon, the body of our dead brother was cut up in chunks and was not quite so troublesome anymore. The last act of that strange liturgy was the buzz of the saw mixing with the rhythmic song of the dancers. Then life went back to normal. The long line of cars got on its way again, leaving behind that wondrous message of life and death.

Science Fiction Trees

Something stirs deep in the human heart in the presence of a dead tree. Mythology, literature and even science fiction make manifest the sacred respect we owe our brothers the trees, sometimes even more profoundly than the commendable efforts of modern ecology. Prominent authors, such as Tolkien, Dino Buzzati, C.S. Lewis and many others, speak of the holiness of trees and their wonderful message with skill and utmost reverence. Sometimes, out of some sense of modesty, they seem to hide their devotion and esteem toward trees in the recesses of imaginary and symbolic tales. Perhaps it is the only way for them to be heard and avoid causing a scandal.

In *The Magic Stones of Shannara*, Terry Brooks describes, through the language of science fiction, the sacred tree of life as immutably perfect. With richly-colored detail, he paints the image of a symmetrical, harmonious form reaching to the sky, a majestic tree, undisfigured by time.

When C.S. Lewis, in the last of his *Narnia Chronicles*, describes the lament of the trees, felled at the height of their lushness, he doubtless creates a beautiful piece of poetry, but something tells us that the weeping of the driad, who seeks justice in the presence of young king Tirian, resonates even today in our collective unconscious. Perhaps more than ever, we are deeply moved as she bemoans the fate of her brothers, "the holy trees", cut down and split open, as more and more of the giant creatures fall to the ground.[2]

The driad's lament reminds me of a scene in a film: the chief of an Indian tribe and his men stare, utterly stunned, at the giant rollers advancing in the Amazonian jungle, swallowing every trace of greenery. I can still hear him cry out in dismay: "Look! They are stripping the earth's skin! How will it be able to breathe?"

Affinity Between Man and Tree

But the message of the trees goes beyond their holiness. Trees have a special way of communicating. They speak.

---

2. C.S. Lewis, *The Last Battle*, Collier Book, New York, 1980, p.16-17

Of course, they do so after their own fashion and at a pace quite different from the hasty way in which we tend to throw words about. You must approach them with humility and a simple heart and you will soon begin to perceive something. There are trees for every taste, every mood and every shade of character: shy, communicative, healthy, sick, distant, romantic, good-natured, wise. Sometimes the communication between man and tree happens spontaneously, through a kind of syntony.

Within a stone's throw of where I am writing, if you climb up the hill of Janiculum, you will find the famous oak of the Italian poet Torquato Tasso. The friendship and affinities that bound them were such that they go beyond the barrier of time. The Romans refer to it as "Tasso's oak", as if it were a member of his family. Now it stands exhausted, afflicted with disease, much as the poet himself when he used to converse with it and dream under its foliage, just before his death. It seems that the oak's ailments began after it was struck by lightening towards the middle of the 19th century. I am very grateful that the English painter A. Strutt managed to paint it right before that catastrophe, thus transforming it into an imperishable memory, together with other famous European trees, collected in his book *Silva Historica.*

This type of symbiosis is perhaps more widespread and commonly practiced in Oriental culture where it acquires even greater spiritual overtones. India's holy men sit under a tree to meditate. The well-known guru A. Elenjimittan once led me to an olive grove and, pointing to the cool shade under the silvery boughs, he said: "This is where they meditate", referring to his disciples. Perhaps most famous is the pagoda fig tree, or *ficus religiosa,* under which the Buddha had his illumination.

In the Bible, we find this same affinity between man and tree as a sign of spiritual elevation: the man of God sits under the oak tree (1Kgs 13, 14). The Lord-Trinity appeared to Abraham by the terebinth of Mamre (Gn 18, 1-15), a tree that became an essential part of trinitarian icons in Eastern Christianity. The prophet Elijah, overcome by mortal anguish, prays to God under a juniper tree (1Kgs 19, 4), and even the Angel of the Lord comes and sits under the terebinth in Ophrah (Jgs 6, 11).

Everyone knows photosynthesis, the mutual exchange that occurs between man and tree on the physical plane: man takes oxygen from the tree and gives it carbon dioxyde, which plants use to manufacture their own food, carbohydrates. However, there is the possibility of another exchange between the two, a conscious one that takes place on a higher plane.

How to Communicate with Trees

In my meditation classes, I invite the participants to experience a special form of communication with trees. The hands serve as both channel and antenna, the palm of the right hand pressed against the trunk of the tree, the palm of the left on the heart. You breath deeply, concentrating on exhaling slowly, as if there were a channel through which the exhaling directed a current going from man to tree. This in itself is an excellent way to understand the tree on a level other than the mental one. However, you will need a certain sensitivity, patience and above all a non-possessive desire to form this kind of friendship with the tree. In order to do this exercise, you must be very relaxed, free of emotional tension, as when trying to be nice to a little animal you do not know yet and who is still shy. This first contact is your introduction, a hand held out to the tree. At this stage of the exercise, you are communicating to the tree, through the exhaling channel, your gentleness and your friendship. The second step consists in inverting the position of the hands, placing the left one on the tree and the right one on the heart, this time focusing on the inhaling. Then, something happens. But it happens imperceptibly and silently, as when on a ferry boat one notices that it is moving only because objects are growing smaller on the shore. By being totally attentive, yet relaxed, you will feel, little by little, that things are not quite as before, that the tree is aware of you and is communicating something. That is it. I will not give assurances or guarantees of any kind, nor behave like some individuals who, provoked by incredulity, reveal their most precious moments which are the safeguard of their inner selves. So, take it or leave it.

God is Watching in the Almond Tree

The message from the trees is most beautifully summed up in the almond tree that Jeremiah sees, while the voice of the Lord comes to awaken him: "What do you see, Jeremiah?" The message is to be vigilant, to be awake, serenely awake, always awake. In Hebrew, almond tree means "watching-tree", because the almond tree is the first to blossom, heralding the arrival of spring. I believe that what is said in the Bible about the vigilant almond tree can be said of all its brothers: they stand erect, as if in constant meditation, immersed in silence, and yet always receptive, open, ready for anything. Truly, God could say about all of them what he says to Jeremiah on the vision of the almond tree:

> "Well have you seen, for I am watching to fulfill my word" (Jer 1, 11-12).
> Behold, God is watching, as in the almond tree, in every tree.

3. MESSAGES OF ABANDON

When Christ wants to underline how important it is not to worry in life, he takes as examples of his teaching two great icons of nature: flowers and birds (Mt 6, 25-34). The essential message these brothers-signs bring to us can be summed up in one word: abandon.

In every religious tradition, there is an attitude of profound relinquishment, of putting oneself in the hands of divine Providence, an attitude which arises spontaneously in human beings only once they have reached a degree of maturity and wisdom in their spiritual growth. First comes ascesis, renunciation, the conquest of virtue, the struggle to overcome our trials... then, all these efforts pale before the one thing that remains: complete abandon.

Wu wei is the classic phrase which in taoism expresses abandon: non-doing, non-acting. But: "The Way is constantly inactive, and yet, there is nothing that does not get done"; "By not acting, there is nothing that is not done" (*Tao Tê Ching,* XXXVII). What a difference with our constant bustling about!

In the Sufi tradition, there is a book in which nothing is written, absolutely nothing. The pages are totally blank. To the Western mind, such a book can only be a joke. And yet the title of this book is *The Book of Books,* indicating that it contains all the wisdom that cannot be expressed in words. If you read it "actively", trying to interpret, to guess, you will go crazy or get furious at the publisher. *The Book of Books* teaches the wisdom of silence and abandon.

Every week, I read the passage from Matthew (6, 25-34) that has brought me light and peace in the vicissitudes of life; in it is also taught the wisdom of abandon.

The "let it be" in taoism, the putting oneself in the hands of Allah praciced by the Muslims, the non-doing of the Yaki Indians, the "letting your prey go" of the Zen tradition are all different modes of the same wisdom that Christ concentrates in two signs of nature: birds and flowers.

Flowers

"Look at the flowers!" It is the best way to understand the wisdom of abandon. If you try to grasp it by dint of reflection and conceptual connections, you will probably rack your brains to no avail and come to the conclusion that it is not for you. Then you will raise all the typical objections of practical, common-sensical people: "What kind of wisdom is this, anyway? Are we supposed to give up, become lazy and inert?"

But the words of the Sermon on the mountain are meant for everyone, they are a gift for everyone, provided we hear them in the right context. Indeed, Christ does not invite us to meditate on how to become lazy in life; he simply says: "Look at the flowers!" In reality, no one looks at flowers.

Once, at the Metropolitan Museum in New York, I was looking at flowers, painted flowers that is, on a magnificent collection of Chinese vases. I was so fascinated by the colors and subtle shades that I took my ball-point and started jotting down on a notebook the different combinations and chromatic effects that I was admiring. I wanted to make sure that I would remember them in the future and, possibly, even attempt to reproduce them. Of course, I proceeded to forget everything, including the notes that I had taken. Years later, I found myself in a meadow, on a break during a retreat. I was completely still, trying to be in tune with the environment, soaking in the peace of that moment. All of a sudden, I looked down. It was spring and small wild flowers were beginning to spring up and cover the ground. I bent down to get a better look. I can still feel the wave of surprise and wonder that washed over me. I was enthralled by two things: the indescribable beauty and harmony of colors that those little flowers were quietly displaying before me, and the fact that it instantly brought back the memory of the Chinese vases at the Metropolitan Museum. I have no intention of drawing comparisons between real flowers and painted ones, nor of pondering the wondrous beauty that lay gratuitously at my feet. Suffice it to say that never before as at that moment had I understood the truth and power of Christ's words: "But I tell you that not even Salomon in all his splendor was clothed like one of them" (Mt 6, 29).

Such is the outcome of the flowers' sweet abandon: beauty and perfect harmony, being attuned to the Whole, including storms, sultry southern winds, dog-day afternoons or dark and cold days.

Look at the flowers: I call upon you, believers and non-believers alike, to try this simple experiment. When you have a problem, especially a complex one, when you are living a situation of conflict that perturbs you, makes you bitter and confused, stretches you to the limit, go outside and look at the flowers. Then summon your courage and wait for the result.

Once, a young monk confessed to me that every day he conversed with a little flower he had discoverd in a garbage can. He had not told anyone (he was German and had been solidly schooled in Aristotelian thought!), but in this unusual way, he had begun to understand, beyond the purely conceptual level, the wisdom of abandon.

The contrast in Christ's words is awesome, almost incredible: "[Wild flowers] do not work or spin... not even Salomon in all his splendor was clothed like one of them". It seems unreal, too poetic to be true. It is almost insulting to those of us who have to struggle every day with computers, endless paper work and chaotic traffic. There does not seem to be another alternative: you either contemplate the flowers or you go on wearing yourself out, trapped in the cage of your own busy scheme of things. True, Jesus does add one small remark directed at the mind: "If God so clothes the grass of the field... will he not much more provide for you, O you of little faith?" But the remark is offered on condition that we first look at the lilies of the field, otherwise it will have little effect. Who will have the faith, the courage and the simplicity that are needed to look at the great sign of the lilies?

Close to the Flowers

I have searched, among the great human models of total abandon, a similarity with the sign of the flowers and the birds. I cannot say that my search was successful. Perhaps Abraham is the best example, then come the patriarchs, the prophets, the saints of simplicity and perfect syntony with nature and Providence, the Fathers of the desert, and, in the non-Christian Orient, the rishis and the sannyasin, genuine taoists, yogis and peaceful zen monks. And yet, to me, none of them appear to be a sign of abandon as obvious and absolute as the flowers and the birds. Abandon in human beings always seems to be incomplete, at least at the onset of the spiritual journey: there always is one step to take from abandon to non-abandon, from the privileges of birth, social position and fortune to the dunes of the desert or the inclement climate of the jungle. And there is always something to "do", renouncing or sacrificing something, or performing some ascetic exercise or applying some yoga techique.

Flowers, on the other hand, never have to go from one point to another or to make sacrifices: they just keep on growing and living as they are, simply open and abandoned, without having to let go of anything, or giving up certain privileges... and yet, they bloom and are perfect!

Also, the human models of abandon that we have seen stubbornly continue to raise queries, in other words, they cannot help involving their rationality which rebels before the mystery of perfect abandon. Abraham has an ongoing dialogue with God and, once in a while, he lets out the incredulous little laughter of a man who has not fully put himself in the hands of God: "Can a child be born to a man who is a hundred years old? Or can Sarah give birth at ninety?" (Gn 17, 17). Moses, while leading God's people through the desert, literally gets fed up of such total abandon and he explodes before God: "Was it I who conceived all this people, or was it I who gave them birth, that you tell me to carry them at my bosom, like a foster father carrying an infant, to the land you have promised under oath to their fathers? Where can I get meat to give to all this people?"

(Nm 11, 12-13). Not to mention the arguments between God and Job, or Jeremiah's regrets and protests in the face of his difficult prophetic mission.

There is nothing wrong in considering these less-than-perfect examples of abandon; they might even encourage us to move forward and help us understand that, after all, we are not that far from them.

As far as flowers are concerned, I do not know any that rebel or complain because the weather is too hot or too cold, or because government laws do not show enough respect for their life. And yet, they are joyful and live without trauma! The paradox, the mystery is hidden in abandon:

The Way is constantly inactive, and yet there is nothing that does not get done...

> "Look at the lilies of the field: they do not work or spin, but not even Salomon in all his splendor was clothed like one of them".

Birds

Never did I contemplate from up close the life of the birds as I was able to do during my stay in Africa. On that afternoon, I was sitting on my small balcony, observing the silent woods. All of a sudden, a whole family of birds (they looked a lot like house-martins, but I am not sure) took over the top of the palm trees that formed a semi-circle right in front of me. In a flash, the scene was transformed into a wonderful ballet. Spread evenly in groups of two or three along the semi-circle, the birds began their dance. It was truly something unique and fascinating! If you are familiar with Russian folk dancing, you will no doubt recall one of its essential choreographic figures: while the corps de ballet, all in a circle, keeps the beat by clapping hands, the principal dancers, one by one, step into the middle to do their pirouettes. In precisely the same way, the birds in pairs would come forward to do their number. They would briefly separate in flight and rise in a breathtaking ascent into the dazzling African sky, almost brushing against each other at the top, then would plunge downward, whirling and twirling, chirping (clearly, they were laughing!), and resume their initial positions to give the next pair its turn. The strange thing was that each couple would perform its dance of jubilation just at the right moment, and not before. It was wonderful to feel their joy at being alive, to admire the complex arrangement of unusual and joyous figures, and the eddying movement of their flight. Truly magnificent.

I think that if I were to lump together all the speeches I have heard in my life and all the books I have read—and there are quite a few—on the subject of "the joy of life", they would not even come close to that marvellous experience conveyed by the message of the dancing tropical birds. There were no lead dancers or maybe they all were. There was no ballet master, no bar, no special techniques, no special costumes, no psychedelic lights, no videos. Only pure joy at being alive. There were no footlights, no orchestra, no public apart from myself, but they knew they were being watched by their one and only spectator. And I knew they knew, and this mutual understanding only seemed to increase their boisterous joy.

One of the participants in the retreat happened to pass by. I asked him about the name of those birds. He did not know, even though he lived in Africa!

I continued watching. I noticed that some of the smaller birds also tried their wings at some aerial feats, but their rather awkward attempts were little more than quick little hops from tree to tree which usually went off without a hitch. Then you would hear an encouraging "Not bad!" from the experienced adults.

When the show was over, I thought of our "civilized" entertainment; it is a true reflection of how we see the joy of life. What complications! Stages require ever more sophisticated equipment to create the appearance of authenticity in such a way as to make the audience forget that it is all artifice. In some avant-garde places, scents are used to create the illusion of a certain environment... everything has to be more and more intense, more violent because it will have no interest for the general public unless it shocks the system. And we can rest assured that we can comfortably enjoy these delights, without worrying about being involved in a global catastrophy, because somewhere in a secret armored chamber, in a secret place, the mighty of the world have hidden enough deadly weapons to balance the fears, tensions and aggressiveness from all sides of humanity.

* * *

It seems that, for now, we still do not find the time to look at the sign of the birds; and yet, in their untiring dance, they unveil to us the secret of the true joy of existing, without specific positions or complicated plans. I guess we must still be too intellectually sophisticated to grasp this mystery of life. Perhaps one day, after so many stupid wars, so much horror and madness, the secret hidden in the sign of flowers and birds will suddenly be revealed to us. And then, as children who have just been initiated to the mysteries of life, we shall understand gloriously and doubt no more. That moment will signal the beginning of our dance.

4. THE THOUSAND VOICES OF THE WOODS

The Offering from the Woods

There are many, many messages that come from the woods, but for me the central one is the great message of offering. To understand it in depth, it is not enough to walk around in the open air and to breath in the oxygen from the trees, nor can this be done in any type of wood. Those in which conifers are dominant, for example, do not convey the sign of offering as richly and as obviously as those at lower altitudes, where conifers grow side by side with birches, ash trees and even oaks, linden and chestnut trees. The undergrowth in these woods is also extremely rich, with a great variety of bushes and aromatic plants that create a multi-textured and multi-colored tapestry. There, the sign of offering is made more manifest in the overall view. All you have to do is sit quietly and look around.

The first time that I perceived the sign of offering, I was completely alone in the middle of a splendid wood of the type just mentioned. I was struck by the presence of the sign. I understood, without needing to reflect, that I was at the heart of a spontaneous liturgy of offering. The oaks were raising their twisted branches as arms that would open and reach for the light. And so did the ferns at their feet, their big leaves unfolded and spread like bright green carpeting cut into a thousand arabesques, each frond ready to receive a passing insect that might alight on it for a moment's rest. Heather grew on my right, its stems covered with countless minute leaves that gracefully unfolded to the light, while their lovely fucshia flowers were offering their best to the worker bees that buzzed around incessantly; after they had collected their precious sweet load, they would fly back to the beehive and offer it as royal food. Even the seemingly less positive details carried the message of universal offering: just a few steps away, as an open invitation to heedless insects, was laid a spider's web. A temptation, but also an offering, an invitation to learn, to grow by overcoming obstacles, taking into account the wisom hidden in the laws and secrets of the woods, which I did not know. Everything spoke the same language: offer, offer, offer. Give like the woods. The pleasure of giving. Keep nothing for yourself. Nothing is yours by exclusive right. Everything is open, everything is available: colors, shapes, perfumes. Even the flaws, the small signs of disease and decomposition, appeared to me as a humble confession, a sincere offering of total straighforwardness, one that is willing to show weaknesses and deficiencies.

I knew then that life too is a continuous offering and that everything opens to us, everything is offered in our existence, just as everything between the creatures of the woods was mutual opening and giving, a constant exchange. Everything is an offering: we either know it or we do not. Sounds, words, encounters, temptations, hardships, the past, the present, the future, the whole of history, it is all offered to us as an invitation to grow in our magnificent human vocation. To become ourselves a living offertory in all things, attuned to the universal offertory of creation, such is our vocation.

The Rules of Walking in Tune with the Woods

Beside this message of offering, there are many others, as rich and varied as there are kinds of woods, depending on their age, size and altitude, on the presence of wild vegetation or of cultivated one, etc. To understand these messages, at least to get an overall view, I advise you to take a very particular walk.

First of all, you must prepare for it. Renzo Baschera has collected the rules that popular wisdom has passed down to all those who enjoy walking in the woods.[3] I will merely point out some of the main ones, adding a few drawn from personal experience.

Silence

To understand the language of the woods, il will be necessary to silence the coarsest, most ordinary sounds, typical of our everyday lives. Thus, it is better not to speak. Even if there are places where collective encounters with nature are encouraged, the higher, more intuitive mystical perception of the language of the woods is usually an individual experience. So walk alone and do not busy your mind, heart and sixth sense with song, poetry or whistling. Let me say it again: this is no ordinary walk. You are in the process of discovering a whole original language, made of extremely subtle sounds, significant silences, changing colors, lights and shadows. Our own silence, humble and

3. R. Baschera, *Magia verde* (Green Magic), Mondadori, Milano, 1990, pp. 141-146.

receptive, will be our best introduction to the woods. If, during your walk, you disrupt the solitude and quiet harmony of the wooded landscape with your common noises, you will spoil everything: the wood will refuse you admittance to the sanctuary of its beautiful language and relegate you to the uninitiated.

Peace

You must not seek the message of the woods on an especially tense day, when you feel overcome by problems and anxiety. The purpose of the walk I am describing is *a new perception of the woods*, not emotional release. Although it is true that nature can understand your need for release and can indeed bring calm and peace to your troubled heart, this is not the time to do it.[4]

An unhurried pace will also favor calm. Without being conditioned by the clock or pre-established goals, simply walk in silence, spontaneously, receptively. Move as naturally and lightly as the creatures of the woods: the branches, the leaves, the insects. Try not to be absent-minded and attune your own particular rhythm to that of the woods. At some point, you might very well feel like stopping to sit for a while, or just standing there, resting in harmony with the peaceful surroundings.

To achieve calm, it helps to be comfortable, so wear good walking shoes and the right clothes for the season.

---

4. To attain calm and purification of the emotional plane, see chap. V of my book *Iniziazione alla preghiera profonda* (An Initiation to Deep Prayer), Edizioni Messaggero, Padova, 1987, pp.50-58.

Solitude

The area of the woods you choose for your walk should be conducive to the mood we have just described. Therefore, it is preferable to go to a more solitary, less popular spot. Places usually crowded are less limpid and are charged with assorted vibrations, not always of a lofty nature. Instead, the solitude and silence typical of less known paths will help you to get in tune with the woods and you will not run the risk of being constantly interrupted and disturbed by the presence of other visitors.

Greeting the Angel of the Woods

The woods, as well as those whose task it is to take care of them and keep them alive, are very sensitive to the psychic state and spiritual dimension of casual visitors. Therefore, it is important to go into the woods with a simple heart and a kind and open attitude toward the invisible catetakers of these beautiful and salutary regions of our planet. When Saint Francis of Assisi went deeply into the woods to pray, the angels gathered around him. The invisible caretakers I just mentioned, these intermediaries between God and human beings, who take many different forms and are revealed in many ways depending on the times and the culture, are called angels in the Christian tradition. But, whatever the form or the interpretation, they all have one feature: invisible angels have a specific task, which is generally the safeguard and the care of creation, including human beings. Within this mission, angels often seek to relate to them, getting them involved in the love and protection of nature and, at the same time, helping them to constantly evolve and fulfill themselves.[5]

I have no doubt that those regions imbued with mystery, such as woods, which naturally elevate the spirit, are entrusted to an invisible guardian angel who sees to their careful protection. I have no desire to go into theological argumentation or anthropomorphic speculations on the particulars of these angelic presences. I will only say that when I visit the woods, I always try to be courteous to them: I congratulate them for the harmonious color arrangements, for the taste and elegance of certain wooded areas, etc. It is just a matter of showing basic courtesy and kindness as we do when we visit friends or acquaintances. Greeting the angel of the woods is a prerequisite to achieving that total and profound syntony with the surroundings which will develop during the walk. We must remember the fundamental principle: the exchange of perception and energy between man and wood is possible only if they are bound by mutual liking.

These preliminary remarks will be sufficient to awaken in most the full and spontaneous syntony with the language of the woods. However, for those who might still be reluctant, I will add some practical and methodological advice that will be useful, especially at the beginning.

---

5. On this subject, see the beautiful book on angels by M.P. Giudici, *Gli angeli. Note esegetiche e spirituali*, Città Nuova, Roma, 1984.

5. THE THREE LEVELS OF THE WOODS

Becoming Attuned to the Heart of the Woods

The woods have an affective dimension, similar to our feelings and emotions. Woodmen, farmers and people who live in the vicinity of the forest are well aware of the variations in its affective life. For example, they observe that nature seems more welcoming on sunny days than on rainy ones. Some tree therapists explain this by saying that, on rainy days or during a storm, the woods tend to close in on themselves to absorb the ambient energy as opposed to giving it off. There is a whole range of possible ways to sense what feelings a paricular wood may have or what its current mood might be.

Perceiving the scents: breath in deeply the aroma of the plants. Sometimes, it is the small plants that awaken this delicate sense in us: lavender, cyclamen, the tiniest moss soaked with moisture whose delicate odor blends with that of old tree trunks... There are dry perfumes, moist ones, cool or hot ones, sweet or bitter, delicate or pervasive...

Perceiving the sounds: the woods play their own symphony every moment of the day. Experts know that there are marked differences between the music of the morning and the melodies of dusk. A times, silence reigns, but it too contains different messages, of expectation or tension, or simply of tranquillity and rest. The most tenuous sounds are sometimes interwoven into the prevailing silence, only to be perceived by someone whose open heart is in perfect tune with the forest. Birds and insects, the wind and the leaves all contribute to the unfolding of the various movements of the symphony, each adding its tempo, vibrations, quiverings, high and low notes. You can clearly hear the soloists, rising above the orchestral ensemble to offer a beautiful aria, full of harmonic flourishes or even monotonous ones, like a sad, continuous humming which eventually fades again into the full sound. We must then try extra hard to be quiet and in complete accordance with our surroundings, maybe by remaining totally still for a while so as not to interrupt the music in progress and spoil its beauty.

Perceiving the colors: the peculiar way in which each wood filters the light and the many shades of color form a splendid paradigm of its current mood. Sometimes the vivid, dazzling colors will suggest a state of exuberant joy. You will be drawn to and surprised by the treasures hidden in the midst of the chromatic tapestry of the the flora: bright hues or subtle half-tones in contrast with the grayish background of the soil and the undergrowth. You will soon have to give up trying to name the infinite variety of original colors of the wild flowers: crimson, deep or electric blue, coral, pearl, purplish... there simply are not enough words in our usual list! You will just have to experience it for yourself!

Once you have achieved syntony with everything around you, let the heart of the wood penetrate ever more deeply inside your own. Let your mood come into play, making sure that it will not bring discord, like a jarring note, into the harmonious whole.

Becoming Attuned to the Forces of the Woods

Beside its heart, the woods possess different energies we shall call "forces". Popular wisdom has many customs and prescriptions to benefit from these forces. Some Oriental practices teach how to absorb the vital energy from plants by placing the palm of the hands or the feet on them. Baths and massages with various plants which, according to tradition, have beneficial effects (rosemary, sage, sunflower...) are often recommended in folk remedies. An ancient prescription suggests that one go and stand every day under a fig tree in order to receive its energy, for the body as well as for the mind. The famous School of Salerno was in agreement in regard to the fig tree, as was the entire Hebrew tradition. The prophet Joel links the abundant blessings from God with the exuberant forces of nature and the vanishing of all fear that should follow:

> Fear not, O land!
> exult and rejoyce!
> for the Lord has done great things.
> Fear not, beasts of the field!
> for the pastures of the plain are green;
> The tree bears its fruit,
> the fig tree and the vine give their yield.
> (Jl 2, 21-22)[6]

It might be useful to recall here what we discussed above on communicating with trees through hand contact. However, I do not wish to give advice of a utilitarian nature on this point. The main thing for personal growth and for a positive and full relation with the environment is to achieve *syntony,* from which will derive friendly exchanges, as opposed to going into the woods to get specific

---

6. For further information on this subject, see the book by Renzo Baschera quoted above.

benefits and never knowing a true harmonious relation with the total surroundings.

To have an overall perception of the forces of the woods, it will help to become aware of our breathing. We have all experienced the urge to breath more consciously and more deeply when we go from the stuffy inside of a vehicle to the fresh and oxygen-rich outdoors. Through the respiratory channels, our being intuitively senses the ambient energy. And wooded areas are especially charged with energy and active ingredients, particles of ether, scents and various organic compounds, which are all absorbed through the breathing process.

So it is most likely that you will stop during your walk and quite instinctively breath in more consciously the atmosphere of the woods, or breath under one particular tree that gives you special energy and from which seem to emanate exceptional strength and solidity: you might sense this by feeling how firmly it is rooted to the ground and how vigorously it shoots up to the sky.

In the summer, you may feel like lying down on the ground. Mother Earth will communicate to you the same mysterious energy and strength which is visibly manifested in the growing vegetation all around you. I must reiterate the importance to take it all in through conscious breathing: you will thus breath Mother Earth's energy and you will have the impression that you are drawing from the very source of the wood's forces.

Becoming Attuned to the Mind of the Woods

It should not be too difficult at this point to understand that the wood possesses a mind as it were, insofar as it forms a harmonious whole, distinct from other regions. In our highly computerized times in which we use all kinds of software to program our machines, we should easily sense that there exists a similar kind of mind that governs the overall life of the woods. Each wood thus carries out a particular task in the great mosaic of the working cosmos. It has a specific mission in a small corner of the planet, and it fulfills it by being precisely the wood that it is supposed to be.

So, go for your walk with the intention of perceiving the mind of the wood in all its different aspects: what do you think is its growth pattern, which way does it face, how able is it to sustain mishaps and bad weather, to absorb, recycle and assimilate various substances, to unfailingly adapt to any circumstance?

The mind of the wood is revealed especially in the sign of order. Observe the wood as a whole: is it not obvious that there is a splendid general order, perfect in its complexity? Let us take traffic in the wood as an example (and there is plenty of it). You will notice that it is infinitely better, more orderly than the traffic in any of our monstruous cities. And yet, it is totally spontaneous and free from tiresome and punitive rules, such as traffic lights and no parking zones. The creatures that live in the wood move harmoniously, according to their own rhythms, as in a dance. Whether they be many or few, they never seem to run about stressed.

A Parade of Butterflies

Once, as I was walking in the African woods, I stopped to listen to the sounds of nature and stood for a while in front of a thick green bush. All of a sudden, a black and white butterfly alighted on it, right in front of me. It was average in size, quite pretty, and it seemed happy and relaxed, not in the least apprehensive about my presence. While I observed it, remaining quite still, I saw another butterfly, exactly like the first one; after having fluttered for a moment over its companion, it came down right next to it. Then came a third, and a fourth one. Before I knew it, a wondrous sight appeared before my eyes. I watched, mesmerized, as ten, twenty, thirty butterflies, dozens, hundreds of them flew calmly and solemnly past, in perfect rhythm, ondulating up and down, in absolute tranquillity and silence. They obviously followed a precise flight pattern, in an orderly fashion yet quite naturally. It always took them right past me, as if they were aware of my amazement. Sometimes, they flew around me, as if suddenly noticing that strange and rare creature in the woods that I was. Some would occasionally pause briefly on the bush, just long enough to show me the delicate filigree of their unfolded wings, and then would take off again, leaving me stunned. When their parade was over, another one began, formed of very beautiful dragon-flies, not in so thick a procession, but in a more fluid and lively one, and especially more brightly-colored: there were blue dragon-flies, yellow ones, black ones...

Parting Reflections

After experiencing these three syntonies, your walk may enter a more analytical and meditative phase: what did my feelings get from the heart of the wood? How did the energy and the forces I sensed all around relate to my deepest energies? How does the mind of the wood enlighten and stimulate my own mind? What is there behind this whole that I perceived, what presence, what hidden messages?

Of course, at the beginning, you will find it more difficult and artificial to establish an authentic friendly rapport with nature. But with practice, it will all come more easily. You just need to be patient and to have a genuine desire to benefit from this new type of communication; with time, you will find that you have at your disposal an entire network of messages which will greatly enrich your existence.

One last piece of advice: clearly, the noble and kind messages and gifts offered by the wood require that you take leave gratefully, courteously and sincerely.

Thus, with a walk in the woods, the wish of an eighteen century German botanist will gradually come true:

When man will learn to speak to the plants anew, he will enter the dimension of wisdom and he shall never fear anything again, not even death.

III

THE SIGNS OF EVERYDAY LIFE

Messengers bring me news
from unknown skies,
they greet me and hasten on their way.
My heart is glad, gentle
is the breath of the passing breeze.

From dawn to dusk
I sit here on my doorstep,
and I know that suddenly
the time will come when I will see.

R. TAGORE

1. GOD PLAYS HIDE-AND-SEEK

I have often heard this story told: God plays hide-and-seek with us. The first time I heard it, it was like receiving a pearl that came to enrich my relationship to others. The Indian master who was telling us the story said to his audience: "Today, God will visit you many times! You will find him in many different ways. When you are at home and when you go out. He will disguise himself as a little old woman, as a bus driver, as a passer-by, as a child and as all the people, known and unknown to you, that you will meet. You must be prepared and always attentive because he will pretend to get angry at you, or to be unkind, or not to understand you, or even to be aggressive. But you will also find him in pleasant disguises, as someone nice and friendly; he will even make you smile and amuse you so that you will forget the horrible disguises. The important thing is that you be determined to find him without hesitation".

It was truly suggestive: God infiltrating humanity clandestinely.[1] But after all, is he not the Emmanuel, God-among-us? Did he not himself tell the same story almost to the letter: "For I was... a stranger and you welcomed me... in prison and you visited me" (Mt 25, 35-36). Perhaps the rules of the game God plays with us arise from the fact that men, especially today, do not like being helped and saved by any one other than themselves, and so God disguises

---

1. In Eastern Christianity, this tradition is well known: God or Christ can visit us any time in the guise of ordinary men, so as to blend in with us, thus the reference to the "clandestine" visitor. See, for example, M. Naimy, *Il libro di Mirdad* (The Book of Mirdad), Ed. Mediterranee, Roma, 1988.

himself as a man. The Indian master called this game "God's thousand disguises", but I think there are many more. This daily game is fascinating and it provides us with wonderful opportunities to elevate our lives to a higher plane and to attain a better understanding of the overall meaning of our pilgrimage. Because the game consists in more than just discovering God under his thousand disguises in every person we meet. It is much richer, more far-reaching. As in boy-scout games, one trail leads to another, revealing new signs in objects as well as in the various circumstances and events of life.

We must not be in a hurry to figure it all out right away, nor must we be anxious about it. Otherwise, what kind of a game would it be? Those who accept the rules must be patient and plunge into the search for signs with a curious mind and a brave heart. Every day, they will surely discover messages that will eventually give them a new vision: the ability to read life spiritually. When the game will have been played to the end, there will be nothing more to guess: that will be the moment of the last and definitive discovery. But that experience is such that it cannot be confined within conceptual terms: it is the great secret to which the game of hide-and-seek leads. Anyone who practices true meditation will eventually feel increasingly drawn to the discovery of this ultimate secret.

God Speaks in our Lives

As Elihu, Job's youngest friend, used to say, God does speak to us, in one way or another (Jb 33, 14), but we do not pay much attention. When he speaks in an extraordinary fashion, almost in an uproar, then man gets frightened; only then does he recognize God's voice: He has spoken!

In this last part of the book, I shall mix different kinds of episodes, things that happened to all sorts of people. But there is one common denominator: every single episode contains a sign-message. I avoid saying "divine sign" on purpose because the spiritual nature of the message is not always obvious in all of the accounts, although in some, it is quite clear. Some of the stories are personal, others are drawn from direct testimonies by participants who attended my meditation retreats. My objective is simple: I want to show everyone that we live constantly surrounded by a most beautiful coded language; there is nothing commonplace about it; it is original, creative, it spurs us on to higher, more transparent levels of existence, far above basic automatisms or collective obsessions that tend to drag us away from this originality and turn us into average consumers, eternally dependent on mass-produced goods, including trendy ideas and conversations.

And if someone should say: "That means living constantly immersed into autosuggestion", I answer that I would rather live my life positively influenced by my own self, in a dimension where I can experience more freely and creatively the marvellous dance that we call human existence, than to be injected, without my knowledge, with all the poisons of the outside world, which in the end debase the person and lead to exhaustion, depression, burn-out and other regrettably well-known neuroses of our times. Besides, it is not really autosuggestion, but a deliberate choice of becoming attuned to one level, as opposed to another, among the many that life has to offer. After all, everyone eventually finds his own rhythm, his own singular way of expressing and living the symphony and of moving in the dance. And I for one am happy to have chosen this one, under the guidance of Ignatius of Loyola, my spiritual father, who tried to be, and taught to be, "contemplative in action" to every man he met, or, as he put it in another way, to know "how to seek and find God in all things".[2]

With the exception of synchronic signs, which I will examine a bit more extensively, I have chosen, for the sake of clarity and simplicity, the shortest of testimonies, each bearing a one-word or key-phrase heading which best expresses and condenses the sign dealt with in each episode. They are but a few samples; the list is endless, since every day brings so many. But they should be sufficient to stimulate interest in someone who is ready to attempt this kind of spiritual reading of everyday life.

2. THE SYNCHRONIC SIGN

Synchronicity

Probably the most burning manifestation of God's presence in our lives is what psychologists call "sychronicity". Some refer to it as coincidence, others prefer to close their eyes and dismiss it altogether.

We owe the concept of synchronicity mainly to C.G. Jung, the famous Swiss psychologist whose important

---

2. Cf. the *Constitutions* of the Company of Jesus, no. 288; the *Autobiography* of Saint Ignatius, no. 30; the *Spiritual Exercises*, nos. 234-237. One of Saint Ignatius' first companions, the Blessed Pierre Favre, was particularly gifted for perceiving and being attuned to the messages from the spiritual dimension of everyday life, as evidenced in his *Confessions,* Pro Sanctitate, Roma, 1980.

body of work is now part of the cultural and scientific heritage of our century. It is mostly in his autobiographical writings[3] that Jung developed his particular theory on signs, supporting it with accounts from his personal life.

Synchronicity means to establisn a significant connection between two or more events that happen simultaneously, which have no cause and effect link, but present themselves somehow connected.

Jung himself experienced some very interesting instances of such synchronicity. One day, one of his patients was telling him a dream in which she was given a gold scarab as a present. At that precise moment, the psychologist was distracted by the sound of an insect dashing against the glass pane. He opened the window and, to his amazement, saw a golden rose-chafer fly in, in other words, that very same species of beetle, with the singular greenish gold shade, which in the summer can be seen on the petals of roses.

Even more striking is the case of pre-cognitive synchronicity that Jung experienced during his meeting with Freud. It is not an over-statement to say that this episode has definite parapsychological overtones.

In *Memories, Dreams, Reflections*, Jung tells us that, one day, while Freud was trying hard to prove to him that parapsychological phenomena were foolish, he began to feel a terrible burning sensation in his diaphragm, as if there were an incandescent iron vault inside him. At that moment, there was the sound of an explosion in the next room, the library. Both men sprang to their feet in terror. Jung felt,

---

3. C.G. Jung, *Memories, Dreams, Reflections,* Random House, New York, 1963.

in a totally irrational fashion, that there would be another one: "To this day, I do not know what made me so sure. But I knew, beyond any doubt, that there would be another bang". He said so to Freud, and sure enough, it happened as he had said. Freud gave him a stunned look, but said nothing, and Jung sensed that he had annoyed him and that Freud had become somewhat mistrustful of him.

Many would simply classify this incident among pre-cognitive telekinetic phenomena, but there is no doubt as to the synchronicity of the two events, Jung's rising tension and burning diaphragm and the explosion in the library.

In his work entitled *Aion*, Jung also presents as an example of synchronicity the coincidence between the historical time of Christ's coming and an objective astronomical event: the start of a new aeon, the age of Pisces.

Synchronicity is thus more than simultaneity, which is the mere juxtaposition of two simultaneous events, not linked in any significant way.

The kind of significance that connects two synchronic events will doubtless always remain ambiguous and mysterious, but one must give credit to Jung for having attempted a courageous scientific evaluation of this phenomenon, one that is all the more meaningful as it comes from a scientist of Jung's calibre, whose absolute honesty in research is above suspicion. And it is because of his honesty that he confesses his inability to explain synchronicity through the omnipotent principle of causality.

His position is also interesting for us as it relates to the scientific evaluation of signs. But beyond this aspect, let us not forget that synchronic signs, as everything else in life, are endowed with a spiritual dimension, and it should be our concern to discover and meditate on this dimension in order to promote the evolution of our spiritual conscience. Moreover, the difficulty of interpretation that the scientist must face when it comes to synchronic events, the ambiguity of their meaning will melt away in the strong light of faith, because the believer knows how to read life as a continuous sign of the One in Whom "we live and move and have our being" (Acts 17, 28). Even if synchronic signs are scientifically related to the non-conscious world, they are nonetheless something that is part of life as a whole. It would thus be absurd to exclude *a priori* our non-conscious world—whether we call it unconscious, subconscious or superconscious—from this whole, this totality of existence permeated with faith.

The Angel of the Four-Leaved Clover

I have personally experienced synchronicity more than once. Perhaps the most astonishing incident of this kind is the one that I attribute to the angel of the four-leaved clover.

It was at the time of the eight-day retreat that every Jesuit must go on once a year. Between meditations, I used to go into the garden. During one of my walks, I do not quite know why, I had the idea of asking the guardian angel of the garden to grant me a gift: finding a four-leaved clover. I wanted to send it to my niece, Maria, a child especially sensitive to the world of plants and with a definite green thumb. So, I walked toward the clover patch and, after carefully looking for a short while, I found a four-leaved clover. There it was, a humble little thing among its brothers, not yet fully grown, shyly unfolding its four leaves without the slightest pride or ostentation, since it hardly seemed to think of itself as something rare. Fascinated and grateful to the angel, I picked the clover and went back to my room to dry it and then send it to Maria as planned. But as I looked at it, I started becoming irritated, disgusted with myself, while at the same time, I felt great tenderness toward the little four-leaved clover that lay exhausted in my hand. What had I done? In my ignorance and haste, I had snatched the life from my little brother, I had taken it from its habitat and cut its life-giving umbelical cord with mother earth that helped him accomplish its special mission on the planet. Saddened by my own stupidity and insensitivity, I went out to the garden again and, in exactly the same spot where I had found it, I replanted the slender stem and prayed the angel, without much hope, to bring it back to life.

But it was all in vain. When, on my next break, I went out to check, the clover was bent even more, evidently lifeless. The day after, it had collapsed and it lay on the ground completely limp, clearly dead. I picked it up again so that it would not decompose, and I put it between the pages of a book to dry. Absent-minded as usual, I forgot in what book I had placed it! As soon as I realized this, I started systematically going through all the books on my shelves, leafing through each one of them, page by page, again and again. I could not forget that the four-leaved clover had been a special gift to me and this spurred me on in my search. To no avail: it had vanished into thin air; I started doubting that the incident had ever taken place and wondered if it was not all a distant dream. And so, I gave up the search and forgot all about it.

One day, as I stood in front of my book shelves, the long-forgotten story of the four-leaved clover popped into my head for no apparent reason. Again, for no particular reason, I suddenly glanced down and was dumbfounded to see there, on the floor, right before me, the delicate, almost transparent form of my dearest brother, the four-leaved clover!

You can well imagine how all my past memories rushed into my mind: my gratitude to the angel for his gift, the frantic search through all the books, my doubts on the authenticity of the occurence, etc.

What you may find even more incredible is the conclusion of this story: I have no idea today where the clover is! It disappeared as fast as it had last appeared. I cannot even remember what I did with it the day that I found it on the floor... I ask myself why it all happened and can only find one explanation: to teach me to always respect nature, to admire it without possessiveness, to love it with detachment.

Indeed, from the very first moment I met the little gift, the dynamics of attachment to the sign, followed by forced, unforseen separation, were repeated again and again like a refrain until the final act.

The synchronicity of the last scene, that is, my sudden, intuitive remembering the four-leaved clover, followed by my finding it on the floor, always carries the same meaning: the story was real, I had not imagined it, but so was the message of detachment—I was supposed to pick the sign, not the clover. I thank the angel of the garden, but I am sorry for Maria.

The Pages of the Breviary

Another curious synchronic sign-event happened to me during a retreat I conducted with a group of nuns. I would always go up to the altar before saying mass to prepare the liturgical texts of the day, either by marking clearly the pages from the big red missal or by choosing a few passages from my breviary. One day, as I was handling the books on the altar as usual, I noticed the nuns were practicing the hymns for the service. At one point, they began to sing a hymn that drew my attention because I especially liked the theme: God is joyful.

And then, two synchronic signs occured consecutively with lightening speed, two wonderful messages: as I leafed rapidly through my breviary, the pages briefly stopped at a postcard with Christ's face on it, which I keep because of a striking look in his eyes. At that precise moment, the words being sung by the nuns, who were totally unaware of the connection, made a reference to the look of God which we can find in the eyes of man. If there had been only that, I could have seen it just as a beautiful coincidence; however, as I leafed through the breviary at the same speed as before (the pace of the singing was as fast as that of the moving pages), it stopped again at another postcard, a small calendar with a picture of Our Lady. I keep it preciously because, in the lower margin, my mother, who did not like to write very often, had written three words: "From your mother". And once again, at that very moment, the singing rose in tune with the second postcard with these words: "A mother's tender love is also a smile from God".

3. THE DOVES OF PEACE

In that same convent, I remember the first time I was received by the Superior. She was quite distressed, but there was something indefinable in her mood that drew my attention. She told me she had just been appointed head of her community, which was torn by conflicts not unusual in the years that followed the Vatican councils. Soon after her arrival, she had also been confirmed in her apprehension that carrying out her new responsibilities would not be easy, nor would it be appreciated by all the nuns. My duty was to lead the group during the eight-day annual retreat.

I tried to comfort her and make some suggestions to help her solve her problems. As I mentioned before, I had noticed something special about her: she was clearly determined to fully assume her responsibilities and to face her new, grievous venture at any cost. I knew of similar cases in which people would have done anything rather than accept the position of Superior, especially in such difficult circumstances. I could not help wondering where she got her energy and her sense of total acceptance without discussion. She probably guessed my silent query since, without my asking, she proceded to tell me her surprising secret.

As soon as she had been advised of her new position by the provincial Superior, she felt a keen desire to refuse well up inside her. Everyone in religious circles knew about the situation of conflict that prevailed in the community to which she had been assigned. Her pain and resentment turned to anguish, desperation, tears. As often happens in the Bible, her dialogue with God became adversarial, almost violent. It is that type of religious dialogue that I call "mad language" and which can be found in the Book of Job.

"On that morning—the nun told me—during the fifteen-minute prayer we have just before noon, I was moaning and crying with God again. I went to the window, knelt down and said to Him: 'O Lord, if it is your will that I accept this heavy responsibility, give me a sign to that effect'. At that very moment, as I watched completely bewildered, two magnificent white doves alighted gently on the window sill".

I wish that I had been there to contemplate the scene, especially the eyes: the look of bewilderment of the sister on her knees, tears still streaming down her face, and that look that doves have, a look of serious innocence.

But the mysterious energy hidden within her, source of her courage and acceptance, was not spent in that one, wondrous sign. The days went by and one morning, the nun was summoned to the porter's lodge; a van had just pulled up to deliver a statue for the garden. It was a Madonna which had been ordered by the former Superior and that the community had been waiting for. You can imagine our sister's surprise when, after the wrapping was removed, she saw a statue of Our Lady holding two white doves! I myself would have had trouble believing it had I not seen the lovely statue, a bit smaller than life, radiating its luminous peace in the middle of the garden.

4. THE LITTLE PROPHET

Although Israel often lamented the fact that there were no more prophets in the land, I tend to believe that they are still among us. It is quite another matter of course whether those who claim to be prophets are the real ones, or whether they always have messages to convey. A clear sign of authenticity has always been the fulfillment of the prophecies, the innocence and transparency of the prophet's life, even his reluctance to be a prophet or his unawareness of being one. I was able to ascertain these signs in a dramatic discovery, which convinced me that, without knowing it, I had been living for years next to a little prophet.

108

In those days, I was a spiritual counselor in a boarding-school for boys. Juan José was about thirteen years old. He was a good, simple, no-nonsense type of boy, endowed with a calm and serenity not commonly associated with teenage effervescence. Because of this quality, I thought he would make a good candidate for the leadership of a local group called "Help and Friendship", a youth organization for High School boys to initiate them to helping the needy. The leader had to call the meetings, give out information, collect the money generously donated by the students from their savings and participate in managing the use of the funds. It was more of a symbolic position, but also an amusing venture inasmuch as it broke the monotony of the school day and provided an opportunity to get genuinely involved.

So, at the end of the year, I sent for Juan José and, without further ado, suggested that he took charge of "Help and Friendship" the following year.

He did not accept right away. In keeping with his character which always led him to reflect before acting, he asked me to kindly allow him a couple of days before giving his answer. Then, things began to happen all at once. Just a few days before exams were finished, I received a note from Juan José in which he informed me that he was ready to accept, but at the same time expressing the fear it might not come to pass. The content of the note seemed a little strange, but in the hectic final days of the term, I did not pay too much attention. Here are his exact words:

Juan José N.N. 4B
Father, in regard to my accepting to take charge of "Help and Friendship" next year, I have absolutely no problem with it. However, it is very likely that I shall not be back next term. Therefore, I think you should consider someone else.

Let me repeat that I would like to be the leader, but I do not deem it possible.

It was only a few weeks later, in the middle of the summer holidays, when I heard the news of his sudden death, that I understood how dramatic and prophetic his words to me had been.

It happened while he was riding through the open fields of the region; he fell from his horse and died instantly, so that he lay down for the last time among the *encinares,* the graceful oak groves that are so common in that part of Spain.

Maybe Juan José had written to me in those terms because he had heard his family talking about the possibility of his going to another school. But this in no way diminishes the power of the prophetic sign contained in the note, written just before he was to leave for a place far more distant than he had expected.

As I write these lines, I have before me Juan José's note. I will always keep it as a little brother, one of the signs of my life. This simple piece of paper indicates clearly that human words can sometimes rise, unbeknown to us, to levels beyond ordinary meaning. The note was written on squared paper, the kind you find in school notebooks, with a red ball-point, red as blood. It is signed "Juan José", the name thrusting upward, while the surname, which means "rock" in Spanish, remains solidly anchored to earth, right below the name. Then there is another charming detail which I will not reveal, but I know that Juan José, the silent little prophet, can see me writing these words and is smiling

5. DREAMS AND SIGNS

I have found among those who practice deep meditation, as opposed to conceptualization, a natural ability for recognizing the signs that come during sleep. These signs are often connected to the divine presence in people's lives. There are countless examples. The two that follow will be sufficient to give a stimulating idea of this particular form of message that begins at the level of dreams.[4]

An Invitation to Dinner

Nadia dreamt about a very handsome young man who invited her to dinner. She told me that the whole atmosphere of the dream was wonderful and that it filled her with joy, making her feel like a little girl in the presence of her host. Moved by a feeling of trusting curiosity, she asked the young man: "O Lord, is it really You?". That is how the dream ended; Nadia woke up and began her day as usual. In the morning, she went to one of the best bookstores in Rome to buy a book. As she was browsing from shelf to shelf, a paper note on the floor caught her attention. She picked it up and immediately found the answer to the question she had asked in her dream. On it were written these words, no doubt inspired from the famous quote from Revelation (3, 20): "You have called me and I have come to dine with you, and you with me".

---

4. On the many ways of interpreting and meditating on the messages from dreams, see my book *Meditare un sogno* (How to Meditate on Dreams), Edizioni Messaggero, Padova, 1989.

The Floating Baby

Someone else who also meditates had this dream: in an atmosphere of silence, peace and profound joy, he saw a father holding his newborn child, all his attention lovingly and joyfully focused on him as he held up the little head that floated above the tranquil and limpid waters of a river. The dreamer could also sense the presence of other friendly figures around the baby, who observed quietly and protected him smilingly. The father's duty was to teach the child the art of living. The idea was to eventually leave him alone in the water, otherwise the child's ability to move and his potential to swim would waste away. And so, very gradually and extremely gently, the father began to let go of the head. Everyone watched in earnest to see how the baby would react and whether he would be able to manage his own movements, thinking he was alone in the middle of the water. At that point, the dreamer saw the baby slowly sinking below the surface. He sank many times, quite unconcerned, as if he did not care if he drowned. In the dream world, there was a growing sense of alarm among the observers, as if they were saying: "If the child only knew how easy it is to move your arms and feet and come up to the surface!". The dream ends here and the dreamer awakes with the absolute certainty that the newborn will learn to swim.

The dream is interesting, especially if taken in the context of what the dreamer was going through at the time, but it would have remained on the level of a beautiful dream parable if it had not been considerably enriched by a sign that came to confirm it the next day. Our man opened a book and read these unexpected words, which I will leave up to the reader to interpret in connection with the dream.

To define the arc of human existence, the Bible uses a significant pair of verbs, "coming-going" (Ps 121, 8). In the passage from one state to another, from one experience to another, is contained the whole of the dynamics of human life. But this movement is bivalent. As for the baby that is born.

As it leaves its mother's womb, it acquires freedom of movement, the autonomy to find its place in the vast, boundless space of the world, but it loses the security, the tranquillity of those months in which everything was assured by the mother, and his hours and his life were parallel to those of the person that had begotten him.[5]

6. GREEN, THE COLOR OF AWAKENING

Kathleen England is a true urban contemplative. Her congregation sent her as a missionary to the Far East, and there she learned the techniques of Oriental meditation. Taiwan, Indonesia, the Philippines and other places in Asia and even in America were for Sister England so many centers of influence to spread her teaching and communicate her own contemplative dimension. That certainly explains that she is extremely open-minded on the subject of meditation. Her universal approach brings her in constant contact with many different social environments and groups of spiritual quest. She not only participates in various meetings and gatherings, but she also offers her services as a consultant and a guide to individuals and reaches,

---

5. Quoted from G. Ravasi, *I profeti* (The Prophets), Àncora, Milano, 1990.

with her writings and her lectures, even scientific and academic circles.

That is why I thought of inviting her when I was asked to organize a series of lectures on meditation in a center in Rome. With her usual generosity, she accepted my invitation and she gave a very original presentation on the value of signs in relation to the experience of meditation. In simple, yet engrossing terms, she related the process that led her to "comtemplation in the city". Here is a brief summary of her talk:

How can one contemplate in the middle of busy streets? To get in touch with the center of our being (God's presence, the original self, etc.) is truly essential, but it can be achieved in many different ways; not just in a monastery or a hermitage, but everywhere and by everyone. It is even possible to do it while going about our daily tasks. I was desperate, distracted by a thousand things. I had to learn the true meaning of attention, of paying attention. But how can one pay attention in such a way that it becomes constant awareness?

I needed a sign, something that could focus my attention to the point of bringing me, if I was ready, to this constant awareness. That is when human psychology came to the rescue. I thought about the power of association and how easily we make use of it, as for example when we tie a knot in a handkerchief to remember something. I decided to do the same, in other words, to find a simple thing that would remind me of being constantly in a state of awareness. The first thing that came to my mind was color: I had to choose a color and then I could easily associate it to remembering to be aware... This way, I would be able to perceive the light hidden behind awareness, which waits there for us to pay attention to it in order to become love.

I chose green, on the spot. But then, what would I do with

this color out on the street? I had to put it to the test. There was no turning back. And so I got started.

As in a chain, every perception of the color green led to anther and, to my great surprise, the whole experience became a case of *embarras du choix.*

Everywhere I looked, I spotted patches of green grass that sprang up between paving stones. I looked around and noticed that the bus stops (now yellow) were all painted green; ads and posters displayed great flashes of green, the buses were green, young people walked by wearing green-patterned shirts or bright green scarves. On another occasion, I was on the sidewalk waiting for a bus that just would not come, feeling somewhat irritated. Not thinking of anything in particular, I looked up and, right there, on the corner of the street, I saw a tree, completely bare with the exception of one graceful twig coverd with leaves.

All these quick invitations to become aware, to stop for a moment and contact the Lord in that "secret place of the heart" through a word, a touch, a look, everything dared me to give an answer. But was it easy?

Did I find the answer to my question and my quest?

In fact, it was not that easy because something strange unleashed a mechanism of refusal within me. Then, the small effort required to enter the "secret place where the Father is", leaving the surface to remain in his Presence for a moment, was unexpectedly confronted by this opposing inner mechanism.

Sheer tenacity helped me to overcome this psychological hurdle, until I finally reached the point where awareness emerged spontaneously and I was able to perceive its signs almost without noticing: countless imperceptible signs leading me to transformation and transcendence.

Behind the color there soon came a special quality of the light that brought me to a deeper perception. I was being guided very gently by the touch of the One who "paints dawn and sunset" and "who lights the flame at the heart of things".

7. YOU ARE NOT ALONE

Amedeo Rotondi relates an incident he personally experienced in Collalto Sabino, a small mountain village
where he had gone to rest and write one of his well-known
works. Having suffered a sunstroke, he was lying in bed,
his head throbbing for the fever, in no shape to write. The
physical pain, the feeling of loneliness and the mental
confusion were such that he thought he might be dying.
However, something clear was on his mind: the certainty
that his guardian angel would never abandon him.

The window was open and he could see the restful
mountainous landscape. And then, the little brother sign
appeared: a small bird came to land on the window sill,
then flew right over to his bed. They exchanged glances,
one of amazement at the unexpected visit, the other of
simplicity and ingenuousness, as the look in a child's eyes.
Then, the exchange became closer, more intense: the bird
let itself be held in the man's hands. Amedeo reflected on
the possible meaning of this strange sign:

> Did the tiny bird perhaps come to help me? How could I be
> sure? And yet I sensed it was so. Indeed, I felt better: the
> confusion in my head had ceased and the ache was now
> faint.[6]

Then it was time to part. Amedeo put the bird down on
the bed, but the little brother would not go. He tried placing
it on the window sill, but the bird still would not leave its

---

6. A. Voldben, *Il protettore invisibile* (The Invisible Protector), Ed. Mediterranee,
Roma, 1992, p. 46.

friend. Finally, Amedeo spoke to it. He wished him to go back to its habitat, amidst the trees and the fresh mountain air, to rejoin the other birds. He spoke as if it could understand him. The little bird-sign stayed a few more minutes, then flew away toward the mountains, vanishing on the boundless horizon. And Amedeo discovered that he no longer felt ill; he grasped the meaning of the message and preserved it forever:

> The memory of the little bird of Collalto has never faded with time; I have always considered it to be a messenger of assistance, of the help that was needed at that moment, a symbol of the exchange that exists in nature between those who love.[7]

8. FREEDOM

Perhaps the most intense sign of freedom that was ever given to me was the dance of a Black African in the middle of the equatorial savannah.

He was old, thin and dirty. His body was covered with sweat and it glistened in the powerful tropical sun. But he went on dancing. He danced in the back of a big truck, loaded with his fellow workers who provided the background.

In fact, I only caught a glimpse of him as I and my travelling companions passed the truck at full speed in our impeccable European car that seemed to fly on the excellent, marvellously straigh roads of the African plains.

---

7. *Ibid.*, p. 47.

But that was enough for me to seize the sign. That body jumping and writhing to the beat of clapping hands, those extended bare arms, those moving hands opening to the vastness of the intensely luminous sky, everything in that man cried out one single message: freedom! freedom!

At the precise moment in which we passed the truck, I looked at him and greeted him with a sign of the hand. He did the same without skipping a beat and smiled at me, showing a single gleaming white tooth that gave his face a strange touch of ancient radiance and joy. We quickly finished passing and the whole scene was left behind, like a dream.

I have heard many a word spoken on freedom, pondered many philosophies and reflections, listened to numerous speeches on the subject. I know *The Declaration of the Rights of Man* adopted by the French Constituent Assembly in 1789 and the *Universal Declaration of Human Rights* proclaimed by the U.N. in Paris in 1948. I have also heard people deplore the lack of freedom, the exploitation of millions of children, and I have heard governments promise to eliminate those situations that threaten freedom. I have seen the symbols of freedom, posters and photographs that serve as constant reminders... And yet, among all my experiences and memories, none has had such an unforgettable impact on me as the image, seen in a flash, of the old African dancing in the sun.

The words of Kalil Gibran come to my mind and these verses from *The Prophet* set themselves around that image, like a poetic frame:

> At the gates of the city and by the fireside
> I have seen you prostrate yourselves
> to worship your freedom.

Just as slaves will grovel before a tyrant
and praise him though he may kill them.
Yes, in the temple grove and in the shadow of the fortress
I have seen the freest amongst you
bear your own freedom as yoke and chain.
And my heart bled inside me;
for you can only be free when
the mere desire to search for freedom
becomes a harness for you,
and when you cease to speak of freedom
as an end and a fulfillment.
You shall be truly free, not when your days
are without toil
and your nights without loss or pain;
but, rather,
when these things enclose your life
and yet, you soar above them,
naked and unfettered.

9. THE HUMAN BODY

To complement the preceding sign with some practical observations, I would like to point out in general the value of the signs that come from our body.

Our entire lives are manifested in our bodies. We are embodied spirits and we express ourselves through our bodies. The body is the natural vehicle of communication for the spirit. Every bodily manifestation has a gestural content and a form, or a significant intentionality. The body of the old African dancer showed simultaneously content and form, that is, his extremities, his rhythmic movements, the expressions on his face, all pointed to one single message of joyful freedom, the fullness of the "here and now" in syntony with the glorious expanse of the savannah, which also radiates unbounded openness and freedom.

At any moment of the day, even while we sleep, our body is constantly emitting televisual messages that say a lot about their director and producer! If human beings do not know how to read their own signs, which are daily, continuous and closest to them, they will waste many opportunities to grow and evolve spiritually. After all, such signs appear for one reason only: to help them know themselves better and understand the meaning and purpose of existence.

From the most distant times of Antiquity, man has always tried to read and understand body signs; moreover, he has used them to express himself and communicate with others on many levels, either to create the first writing characters or in gestural languages at a distance.

Illness can be read this way, as a manifestation of some inner disorder. Many Faculties of Medicine and Psychology have developed the study and classification of body signs, giving rise to new scientific disciplines such as chirology and physiognomy. I know an eminent psychiatrist, Dr. Paolo Aite, who uses an original therapy which emphasizes observing the gestures of the patients, who are also encouraged to play and express themselves by moulding shapes with colored sand.[8] Psychosomatic medicine and the less known approach advocated by the German psychotherapist Thorwald Dethlefsen and Dr. Rüdiger Dahlke both have as their premise the reading of body signs

---

8. Cf. P. Aite, *Sognando con le mani* (Dreaming With Your Hands), "Rivista di psicologia analitica", 41, 1990, pp.35-52.

which, if appropriately interpreted and treated, contribute to the health and fulfillment of the whole individual.[9]

Furthermore, even though this particular way of looking at illness, clearly setting aside the religious plane, does not fully coincide with the Christian concept of suffering, which cannot be limited only to the symptoms, it is not too far removed from the thought of Paul: he urges us to consider suffering as part of our experience as we grow in our mystical union with Christ. In his letter to the Hebrews, he writes that Christ "learned obedience from what he suffered" (Heb 5, 8), in other words, he learned to be in tune with the Father's design, and so, "when he was made perfect, he became the source of eternal salvation for all who obey him" (Heb 5, 9). Thus, as Paul puts it, a Christian completes in his flesh what is lacking in the afflictions of Christ (cf. Col 1, 24) and, learning as Christ did from what he suffers, he moves toward the fullness of the whole mystical body of Christ.

According to the authors mentioned above, a physical symptom reveals what is lacking in someone in order to fulfill his purpose, which is to develop toward fullness of being. A symptom is thus a sign of the spirit, which sends its message by embodying itself, making itself visible in it. True healing can only occur if one takes into account the constant striving toward spiritual fulfillment. And so, in keeping with this therapeutic principle, faced with a particular symptom, man must confront and live what is lacking in his awareness and, by doing so, he will grow and heal.

---

9. T. Dethlefsen—R. Dahlke, *Malattia e destino* (Illness and Destiny), Ed. Mediterranee, Roma, 1986.

Any kind of inflammation, stomach upsets, headaches, respiratory problems, skin rashes, etc. are so many signs one must be aware of and which should prompt us to ask: "What does this sign from my body prevent me from doing?" or: "What is it telling me to do?".

Going even further along these lines, we can say that our body also manifests its victories and shows us with positive signs if it is growing toward self-realization and plenitude. Above all, it expresses love, light and life, the ultimate purpose of our existence. In his beautiful verses, Fariduddin Attar expresses most strikingly the fundamental attitude of continuously expanding awareness which human beings must adopt in order to read accurately their body signs:

> You said:
> "Which sign points the way, O dervish?"
> Listen, then,
> and when you have listened, meditate!
> This is the sign for you:
> that you, though you go forward
> shall see your woes ever increasing![10]

---

10. Quoted by T. Dethlefsen—R. Dahlke in *op. cit.*,p. 108.

CONCLUSION

The lamp of the body is your eye.

LUKE 11, 34

When one writes a book, one is never alone. Even though my door is closed and it is a time of day when no unforseen disturbances or telephone rings will disrupt the quiet, I feel close to you, here and now, in constant communication with whomever reads me. I am sure that all those who have something to say, and actually write it, feel the same way.

It is precisely because of this connection with you that I have at times sensed your doubts and difficulties. And now that the book is nearly completed, I can still hear some mild objections coming from you, probably from those who tend to read haphazardly, just leafing through the book, reading one page here, one page there, more or less interested in the subject, and then say: "That is all very nice, but I do not have the time to practice it". To which I would answer: "It is not so much that you do not have the time, you do not have the eyes for it!" "When your eye is sound,—says Jesus—then your whole body is filled with light... then it will be as full of light as a lamp illuminating you with its brightness" (Lk 11, 33-36). My goal in this book was not to push my readers to strain their sight in order to look for signs at any cost. It is important to understand that everyone sees life according to the clarity of his vision. And of course, when I speak of "eyes" and "vision", I am referring to anything that helps people to perceive life and not just to one of our senses.

It does happen on the physical level. The naked eye can only see certain shapes and colors. But if, for example, you observe a piece of mineral in ultraviolet light, the neutral shade of the rock containing the mineral will become luminous and shimmering. Besides, everyone knows that the blue color of the sky on a cloudless day comes from the light being reflected by all the particles suspended in space. It is therefore an optical illusion, or if you prefer, a way of seeing reality in keeping with the present capability of the human eye, which would doubtless perceive reality differently if it were equipped with an electronic microscope.

In this sense, I do not think that there is a life "with" or "without" signs, but rather eyes that can see more or less at different levels of our being, depending on how limpid they are. The eye is the key to all the reflections and the testimonies offered in these pages. It is the eye, the great big eye that a human being open to life is, that will focus spontaneously on what it is interested in seeing and seizing, and only on that. Right now, I can hear the sound of an ambulance siren rushing through the busy streets of Rome. If I want to, I can continue to perceive it, and attune all my thoughts and feelings, and even my actions, to that sound. But I can also block it out if I want to, because I have to work on my book and that appeals to me; so I choose to concentrate on my light green squared paper and I cheerfully let the dark blue ink of my microliner flow across the pages.

There are but a few who can see. Some never even perceive a minute portion of all they could see in life, and they behave accordingly. Go out in the street and you will know what I mean about the condition of people's vision. Observe everyone, men, women, children, young and old: some only have eyes for shop windows, others only for the young man or young woman walking beside them, others move like robots as soon as the light changes, others will even walk looking backwards. But you will be able to tell from the look in their eyes that many are trapped, hypno-

126

tized by their problems which interfere with their ability to see life clearly, and that they move only out of a sort of inertia, more or less disconnected from everything around them.

Yogananda, the famous Indian guru, tells us that once he was in Mexico, visiting the "Floating Gardens" of Xochimilco lake, which in those days were not yet fixed islands. As he gazed at the beautiful sight, he felt enraptured and uplifted, perfectly attuned to the divine Artist, author of such wonders. Next to him, another visitor seemed equally absorbed in the view. But when Yogananda asked him what he was feeling, the man answered: "I was trying to figure out a way to drain the lake to reclaim land". He was an engineer and only saw life in technical terms.[1]

And that is the meaning of these pages: an invitation to keep your antennas well polished to tune into the reality of your own existence more and more fully, to gaze at it with shining eyes, for "if your eye is sound", everything will be "filled with light".

An invitation to look at life with limpid eyes; I never claimed to make a theological study of signs, or an analysis of the signs of the times, or a pastoral commentary on the liturgy of the sacraments, the signs of salvation. All these topics have already been amply and excellently discussed by specialists.

I simply wanted to stimulate your curiosity and urge you to take that first step, which might be to ask yourself: "Is it really possible that everything should be filled with light"? Then, little by little, you will awaken from your

---

1. Paramahansa Yogananda, *L'eterna ricerca dell'uomo* (Man's Eternal Quest), Astrolabio, Roma, 1980, p. 251.

drowsiness, open your eyes; you might even feel the need to cleanse them, as a child who wakes up in the morning has the urge to rub his eyes, and then looks out the window. Then you will surely smile and exclaim: "What a beautiful day!".

Printed in Canada

Métrolitho
Sherbrooke, Quebec